CONTEMPORARY LITERATURE
AND THE LIFE OF FAITH

Listening
FOR God

Volume 3

Contributing Editors

Paula J. Carlson

Peter S. Hawkins

Augsburg Fortress
MINNEAPOLIS

LISTENING FOR GOD, Volume 3
Contemporary Literature and the Life of Faith

This Reader is accompanied by a Leader Guide.

Production made possible in part by a grant from the Louisville Institute, Louisville, Kentucky.

Cover painting: "My South Pond" by James Wilcox Dimmers. Copyright © James Wilcox Dimmers. Used by permission.

Editors: Heather Eeman Hammond and Carolyn F. Lystig

The Library of Congress has cataloged volume one as follows:

Listening for God : contemporary literature and the life of faith /
    contributing editors, Paula J. Carlson, Pater S. Hawkins
        p.   cm
    ISBN 0-8066-2715-8
    1. American literature—Christian authors.   2. Christian life—
Literary collections.   3. American literature—20th century.
4. Faith—Literary collections.   I. Carlson, Paula J.   II. Hawkins, Peter S.
PS508.C54L57   1994
813'.54080382—dc20   96-50662
                                                                              CIP

Manufactured in the U.S.A.   ISBN 0-8066-3962-8   AF 10-39628

03   02   01   00   1   2   3   4   5   6   7   8   9   10

Contents

Acknowledgments

"The Five-Forty-Eight" from *The Stories of John Cheever* by John Cheever. Copyright © 1954 by John Cheever. Reprinted by permission of Alfred A. Knopf, Inc. and Random House UK Limited. Published in the UK by Jonathan Cape.

"Mrs. Cassidy's Last Year" from *Temporary Shelter: Short Stories* by Mary Gordon. Copyright © 1987 by Mary Gordon. Reprinted by permission of Random House, Inc. and Sterling Lord Literistic, Inc.

"Pray without Ceasing" from *Fidelity: Five Stories* by Wendell Berry. Copyright © 1992 by Wendell Berry. Reprinted by permission of Pantheon Books, a division of Random House, Inc.

"Christmas 1967" from *Mr. Ives' Christmas* by Oscar Hijuelos. Copyright © 1995 by Oscar Hijuelos. Reprinted by permission of HarperCollins Publishers, Inc. and Harriet Wasserman Literary Agency.

"Long Night" from *The Collected Short Stories* by Reynolds Price. Copyright © 1993 by Reynolds Price. Reprinted by permission of Scribner, a division of Simon & Schuster, Inc.

"Satan: Hijacker of a Planet" by Louise Erdrich from *The Atlantic Monthly* 280, no. 2 (August 1997): 64-68. Copyright © Louise Erdrich. Reprinted by permission.

"The Woman Who Prayed" from *At the Owl Woman Saloon* by Tess Gallagher. Copyright © 1997 by Tess Gallagher. Reprinted by permission of Scribner, a division of Simon & Schuster, Inc. and ICM.

"O Yes" from *Tell Me a Riddle* by Tillie Olsen. Copyright © 1956, 1957, 1960, 1961 by Tillie Olsen. Reprinted by permission of Dell Publishing. Used by permission of Delacorte Press/Seymour Lawrence, a division of Random House, Inc. and Elaine Markson Agency.

Introduction

When Paula Carlson and I first conceived of *Listening for God: Contemporary Literature and the Life of Faith*—a reader sampling of some of the finest prose writers of our time—we had no idea if the resource would find its target audience. We knew that faith communities were accustomed to turning to Scripture for nourishment, as well as to the slew of inspirational guides that fill the shelves of chain bookstores as well as of religious bookstores. We also knew that there was a market for anthologies of all kinds. However, what would the faithful make of essays and stories that kept you guessing and preferred to drop hints rather than make points? How would they take to writing that demanded close attention, that does not give up its treasures to the first or to the fast read? And what if the writers in question represented any number of connections to the Christian tradition—or even held it at arm's length?

With two volumes of *Listening for God* now behind us, we can see that our uncertainty about the venture did not take into account the sophistication of our readers. Responses have come from a variety of quarters—not only the parish study groups for which we originally wrote, but also from college chaplaincies, literature classrooms, library book clubs, and the individuals who simply stumbled on one or the other volume and found they could not put it down. It would seem from sales as well as from frequent reports that the concept of *Listening for God* has successfully found its audience: people who appreciate technically accomplished writing, who find it stimulating for thinking deeply about faith concerns, and who relish the variety represented in our authors.

In this third volume, for instance, we have writers who range in age from 88 to 46. The geographical settings of their work span much of the United States. Reynolds Price and Wendell Berry locate their imaginations primarily in the upper South (although in "Long Night" Price takes us to Bethlehem instead of North Carolina. Tess Gallagher places her characters in the Pacific Northwest; Louise Erdrich in the Dakotas; and Tillie Olsen in San Francisco. Metropolitan New York is represented by three of our contributors—John Cheever, Mary Gordon, and Oscar Hijuelos—each of whom creates quite a different urban milieu.

Christianity also figures variously in these fictions. Olsen and Price give us outsiders looking in, struggling to understand what is real in a spiritually foreign world. On the other hand, the characters we find in Berry's "Port William," or in Hijuelos's "Upper West Side," are suffused with faith and marked by the peculiar anguish that befalls believers. Some pray without ceasing, others only when death seems imminent or the familiar world falls apart.

Our hope for this volume is that it will continue to provoke the stimulation our readers have enjoyed in the past. In particular, we hope that these fictions open the way for faith discussions that move participants beyond guarded affirmations or predictable platitudes. Our stories have little patience with what is prepackaged or unambiguous. They aim to unsettle, to stir up emotions rather than quiet them down. We recall the impact of stories like Raymond Carver's "A Small Good Thing" or Andre Dubus's "A Father's Story" or Frederick Buechner's "The Dwarves in the Stable"—stories (included in volume 1) where family loss defies any pious response and ambiguous situations remain ambiguous.

Our readers tell us that while preachers and theologians can speak eloquently about the impact of grace on a life, the stakes seem so much more compelling when grace comes hurling across the room in Flannery O'Connor's "Revelation" or is felt in the silences explored by Annie Dillard or Kathleen Norris, all stories included in volume 2. Now volume 3, in its turn, brings forth its own literary treasures—more opportunities to discover anew the mystery of God in some of the best writing being done in North America today.

Peter S. Hawkins

1

John Cheever

Although John Cheever was acclaimed for the five novels he published before his death in 1982, it will most probably be his short stories that secure his place in literature. Sixty-one of these stories (most originally published in *The New Yorker* magazine), the work of three decades, were collected in a 1979 volume that won both the Pulitzer and the National Book Critics Awards, *The Stories of John Cheever*. Collectively they present a distinctive fictional world—Cheever Country.

Postwar and affluent, situated on Manhattan's Upper East Side or in the northern Westchester suburbs, it is peopled by White, Anglo-Saxon, Protestant men who ride commuter trains to their city offices, by women who stay at home and wait for the first cocktail of evening, and by children kept busy with dancing class, horse-riding lessons, and parental mayhem. Gin flows freely and usually to disastrous effect. There is pervasive worry about maintaining a standard of living that was either inherited or only recently acquired; likewise an undercurrent of anxiety about fitting in, looking good, and staying young: "[Cash Bentley] has been adored and happy and full of animal spirits, and now he stands in a dark kitchen, deprived of athletic prowess, his impetuousness, his good looks—of everything that means anything to him" ("O Youth and Beauty!").[1] Cheever's characters are haunted by disappointment and regret, puzzled by feelings and events bewilderingly gone awry. They are also nostalgic for a richer past, one not only based on sounder morals but also more securely "comfortable." For despite the many fortifications of upper-middle-class life, the affair always ends badly, the marriage unravels, and the "boarding school virtues" of "courage, good sportsmanship, chastity, and honor" ("The Bus to St. James's")[2] collapse under pressure. The bonhomie of the ubiquitous cocktail party melts like the ice in a glass of Scotch.

However accurate this thematic summary may be, it does not do justice to the artistic craft of Cheever's fiction, especially to his minute observation of the social reality of Fifth Avenue apartments or Shady Hill. A home in that leafy suburb, for instance, is "not the kind of household where, after prying open a stuck cigarette box, you would find a shirt button and a tarnished nickel" ("The Country Husband").[3] Early evening is "that hour in the suburbs when the telephone rings steadily with board-meeting announcements, scraps of gossip, fund-raising pleas, and invitations" ("Just Tell Me Who it Was").[4] A pretentious woman fails in her disguise: "the seraphic look she assumed when she listened to music was the look of someone trying to recall an old telephone number" ("An Educated American Woman").[5] A beleaguered husband returns to a house of sick children and a wife at wit's end: "it stank of cough syrup and tobacco, fruit cores and sickbeds" ("The Season of Divorce").[6]

Christianity plays some vestigial role in Cheever Country: the local rector is on the cocktail party circuit, children say the Lord's Prayer before going to sleep, and not even a Saturday night hangover cancels the eleven o'clock service at Christ Church. Still, the connection to faith is tenuous: "Cash sang, prayed, and got to his knees, but the most he ever felt in church was that he stood outside the reality of God's infinite mercy, and, to tell the truth, he no more believed in the Father, the Son, and the Holy Ghost than does my bull terrier" ("O Youth and Beauty!").[7] Cheever himself, on the other hand, was a practicing Episcopalian who went to church to "make his thanksgivings"[8] and because, in the end, there has to be someone you thank for the party. His posthumously published *Journals* reveal the depth of his somewhat tortured faith, and the degree to which eventually he found in Alcoholics Anonymous, a fervor missing from the traditional corporate worship he otherwise preferred.[9]

Cheever's preface to his collected stories claims that the constants in his work are "a love of light and a determination to trace some moral chain of being").[10] However foggily, his characters recognize that they have been expelled from Eden yet long nonetheless for the luminous Garden they can still, somehow, recall. No matter how dark the setting, in other words, there is a deep longing for the radiance of spiritual light: "One not only needs it, one struggles for it. It seems to me almost that one's total experience is the drive toward light. Or, in the case of the successful degenerate, the drive into an ultimate darkness, which presumably will result in light."[11]

"The Five-Forty-Eight" presents one such successful degenerate whose drive into darkness may or may not issue forth into light. This story, like "The Swimmer," is one of Cheever's most renowned, inspiring Raymond Carver's sequel, "The Train," and a PBS adaptation by Terrence McNally. Many of the familiar features of Cheever Country are here: a familiar world of offices and trains, calendars and commuter schedules, abandoned wives and adulterous husbands. And yet injected into this realistic setting are elements of fable. Blake is all but inhuman in his cruelty and control, his wronged secretary ("Miss Dent, Miss Bent, Miss Lent") is either a Fury or an Avenging Angel, and the banal surroundings of train car and station are transformed into the place of divine Judgment: "Destruction and death say we have heard the force with our ears." In effect calling his suburban world to account, Cheever takes one particularly arrogant citizen of Shady Hill and plunges him into a darkness that corresponds to his interior state; he puts a gun to his head, and rubs his face in the dirt from which we all come and to which we all return. The question remains, who will Blake be when he raises himself up from the dust and makes his way home? What place will he occupy on the "moral chain of being"?

Peter S. Hawkins

Notes

1. John Cheever, *The Stories of John Cheever* (New York: Alfred A. Knopf, 1978), 216.

2. Ibid., 271.

3. Ibid., 326.

4. Ibid., 383.

5. Ibid., 523.

6. Ibid., 141.

7. Ibid., 217.

8. "I go to church to make my thanksgivings. Period. The level of introspection I enjoy on my knees is something I enjoy nowhere else." Susan Cheever Cowley, "A Duet of Cheevers/1977" in *Newsweek*, (14 March 1977): 68-73. In *Home Before Dark* (Boston: Houghton Mifflin, 1984), 168, Susan Cheever recalls that her father's "religious requirements" were "that the service come from Cranmer's rite in the old Prayer Book, that it take thirty-three minutes or less, that the church be within ten minutes' driving distance, and that the altar be sufficiently simple so it would not remind him of a gift shop."

9. "I do observe how loudly and with what feeling we say the Lord's Prayer in these unordained gatherings. The walls of churches have not for centuries heard prayers said with such feeling." *The Journals of John Cheever*, edited by Benjamin Cheever (New York: Alfred A. Knopf, 1991), 320.

10. Cheever, *Stories*, vii.

11. John Hersey, "Talk with John Cheever" in *Conversations with John Cheever* (Jackson, Miss.: University Press of Mississippi, 1987), 120.

The Five-Forty-Eight

When Blake stepped out of the elevator, he saw her. A few people, mostly men waiting for girls, stood in the lobby watching the elevator doors. She was among them. As he saw her, her face took on a look of such loathing and purpose that he realized she had been waiting for him. He did not approach her. She had no legitimate business with him. They had nothing to say. He turned and walked toward the glass doors at the end of the lobby, feeling that faint guilt and bewilderment we experience when we bypass some old friend or classmate who seems threadbare, or sick, or miserable in some other way. It was five-eighteen by the clock in the Western Union office. He could catch the express. As he waited his turn at the revolving doors, he saw that it was still raining. It had been raining all day, and he noticed now how much louder the rain made the noises of the street. Outside, he started walking briskly east toward Madison Avenue. Traffic was tied up, and horns were blowing urgently on a crosstown street in the distance. The sidewalk was crowded. He wondered what she had hoped to gain by a glimpse of him coming out of the office building at the end of the day. Then he wondered if she was following him.

Walking in the city, we seldom turn and look back. The habit restrained Blake. He listened for a minute—foolishly—as he walked, as if he could distinguish her footsteps from the worlds of sound in the city at the end of a rainy day. Then he noticed, ahead of him on the other side of the street, a break in the wall of buildings. Something had been torn down; something was being put up, but the steel structure had only just risen above the sidewalk fence and daylight poured through the gap. Blake stopped opposite here and looked into a store window. It was a decorator's or an auctioneer's. The window was arranged like a room in which people live and entertain their friends. There were cups on the coffee table, magazines to read, and flowers in the vases, but the flowers were dead and the cups were empty and the guests had not come. In the plate glass, Blake saw a clear reflection of himself and the crowds that were passing, like shadows, at his back. Then he saw her image—so close to him that it shocked him. She was standing only a foot or two behind him. He could have turned then and asked her what she wanted, but instead of recognizing her, he shied away abruptly from the reflection of her contorted face and went along the street. She might be meaning to do him harm—she might be meaning to kill him.

The suddenness with which he moved when he saw the reflection of her face tipped the water out of his hat brim in such a way that some of it ran down his neck. It felt unpleasantly like the sweat of fear. Then the cold water falling into his face and onto his bare hands, the rancid smell of the wet gutters and paving, the knowledge that his feet were beginning to get wet and that he might catch cold—all the common discomforts of walking in the rain—seemed to heighten the menace of his pursuer and to give him a morbid consciousness of his own physicalness and of the ease with which he could be hurt. He could see ahead of him the corner of Madison Avenue, where the lights were brighter. He felt that if he could get to Madison Avenue he would be all right. At the corner, there was a bakery shop with two entrances, and he went in by the door on the crosstown street, bought a coffee ring, like any other commuter, and went out the Madison Avenue door. As he started down Madison Avenue, he saw her waiting for him by a hut where newspapers were sold.

She was not clever. She would be easy to shake. He could get into a taxi by one door and leave by the other. He could speak to a policeman. He could run—although he was afraid that if he did run, it might precipitate the violence he now felt sure she had planned. He was approaching a part of the city that he knew well and where the maze of street-level and underground passages, elevator banks, and crowded lobbies made it easy for a man to lose a pursuer. The thought of this, and a whiff of sugary warmth from the coffee ring, cheered him. It was absurd to imagine being harmed on a crowded street. She was foolish, misled, lonely perhaps—that was all it could amount to. He was an insignificant man, and there was no point in anyone's following him from his office to the station. He knew no secrets of any consequence. The reports in his briefcase had no bearing on war, peace, the dope traffic, the hydrogen bomb, or any of the other international skulduggeries that he associated with pursuers, men in trench coats, and wet sidewalks. Then he saw ahead of him the door of a men's bar. Oh, it was so simple!

He ordered a Gibson and shouldered his way in between two other men at the bar, so that if she should be watching from the window she would lose sight of him. The place was crowded with commuters putting down a drink before the ride home. They had brought in on their clothes—on their shoes and umbrellas—the rancid smell of the wet dusk outside, but Blake began to relax as soon as he tasted his Gibson and looked around at the common, mostly not-young faces that surrounded him and that were worried, if they were worried at all, about tax rates and who would be put in charge of merchandising. He tried to remember her name—Miss Dent, Miss Bent, Miss Lent—and he was surprised to find that he could not remember it, although he was proud of the retentiveness and reach of his memory and it had only been six months ago.

Personnel had sent her up one afternoon—he was looking for a secretary. He saw a dark woman—in her twenties, perhaps—who was slender and shy. Her dress was simple her figure was not much, one of her stockings was crooked, but her voice was soft and he had been willing to try her out. After she had been working for him a few days, she told him that she had been in the hospital for eight months and that it had been hard after this for her to find work, and she wanted to thank him for giving her a chance. Her hair was dark, her eyes were dark; she left with him a pleasant impression of darkness. As he got to know her better, he felt that she was oversensitive and, as a consequence, lonely. Once, when she was speaking to him of what she imagined his life to be—full of friendships, money, and a large and loving family—he had thought he recognized a peculiar feeling of deprivation. She seemed to imagine the lives of the rest of the world to be more brilliant than they were. Once, she had put a rose on his desk, and he had dropped it into the wastebasket. "I don't like roses," he told her.

She had been competent, punctual, and a good typist, and he had found only one thing in her that he could object to—her handwriting. He could not associate the crudeness of her handwriting with her appearance. He would have expected her to write a rounded backhand, and in her writing there were intermittent traces of this, mixed with clumsy printing. Her writing gave him the feeling that she had been the victim of some inner—some emotional—conflict that had in its violence broken the continuity of the lines she was able to make on paper. When she had been working for him three weeks—no longer—they stayed late one night and he offered, after work, to buy her a drink. "If you really want a drink," she said, "I have some whiskey at my place."

She lived in a room that seemed to him like a closet. There were suit boxes and hatboxes piled in a corner, and although the room seemed hardly big enough to hold the bed, the dresser, and the chair he sat in, there was an upright piano against one wall, with a book of Beethoven sonatas on the rack. She gave him a drink and said that she was going to put on something more comfortable. He urged her to; that was, after all, what he had come for. If he had any qualms, they would have been practical. Her diffidence, the feeling of deprivation in her point of view, promised to protect him from any consequences. Most of the many women he had known had been picked for their lack of self-esteem.

When he put on his clothes again, an hour or so later, she was weeping. He felt too contented and warm and sleepy to worry much about her tears.

As he was dressing, he noticed on the dresser a note she had written to a cleaning woman. The only light came from the bathroom—the door was ajar—and in this half light the hideously scrawled letters again seemed entirely wrong for her, and as if they must be the handwriting of some other and very gross woman. The next day, he did what he felt was the only sensible thing. When she was out for lunch, he called personnel and asked them to fire her. Then he took the afternoon off. A few days later, she came to the office, asking to see him. He told the switchboard girl not to let her in. He had not seen her again until this evening.

Blake drank a second Gibson and saw by the clock that he had missed the express. He would get the local—the five-forty-eight. When he left the bar the sky was still light; it was still raining. He looked carefully up and down the street and saw that the poor woman had gone. Once or twice, he looked over his shoulder, walking to the station, but he seemed to be safe. He was still not quite himself, he realized, because he had left his coffee ring at the bar, and he was not a man who forgot things. This lapse of memory pained him.

He bought a paper. The local was only half full when he boarded it, and he got a seat on the river side and took off his raincoat. He was a slender man with brown hair—undistinguished in every way, unless you could have divined in his pallor or his gray eyes his unpleasant tastes. He dressed—like the rest of us—as if he admitted the existence of sumptuary laws. His raincoat was the pale buff color of a mushroom. His hat was dark brown; so was his suit. Except for the few bright threads in his necktie, there was a scrupulous lack of color in his clothing that seemed protective.

He looked around the car for neighbors. Mrs. Compton was several seats in front of him, to the right. She smiled, but her smile was fleeting. It died swiftly and horribly. Mr. Watkins was directly in front of Blake. Mr. Watkins needed a haircut, and he had broken the sumptuary laws; he was wearing a corduroy jacket. He and Blake had quarreled, so they did not speak.

The swift death of Mrs. Compton's smile did not affect Blake at all. The Comptons lived in the house next to the Blakes, and Mrs. Compton had never understood the importance of minding her own business. Louise Blake took her troubles to Mrs. Compton, Blake knew, and instead of discouraging her crying jags, Mrs. Compton had come to imagine herself a sort of confessor and had developed a lively curiosity about the Blakes' intimate affairs. She had probably been given an account of their most recent quarrel. Blake had come home one night, overworked and tired, and had found that Louise had done nothing about getting supper. He had gone into the kitchen, followed by Louise, and had pointed out to her that the date was the fifth. He had drawn a circle around the date on the kitchen calendar. "One week is the twelfth," he had said. "Two weeks will be the nineteenth." He drew a circle around the nineteenth. "I'm not going to speak to you for two weeks," he had said. "That will be the nineteenth." She had wept, she had protested, but it had been eight or ten years since she had been able to touch him with her entreaties. Louise had got old. Now the lines in her face were ineradicable, and when she clapped her glasses onto her nose to read the evening paper, she looked to him like an unpleasant stranger. The physical charms that had been her only attraction were gone. It had been nine years since Blake had built a bookshelf in the doorway that connected their rooms and had fitted into the bookshelf wooden doors that could be locked, since he did not want the children to see his books. But their prolonged estrangement didn't seem remarkable to Blake. He had quarreled with his wife, but so did every other man born of woman. It was human nature. In any place where you can hear their voices—a hotel courtyard, an air shaft, a street on a summer evening—you will hear harsh words.

The hard feeling between Blake and Mr. Watkins also had to do with Blake's family, but it was not as serious or as troublesome as what lay behind Mrs. Compton's fleeting smile. The Watkinses rented. Mr. Watkins broke the sumptuary laws day after day—he once went to the eight-fourteen in a pair of sandals—and he made his living as a commercial artist. Blake's oldest son—Charlie was fourteen—had made friends with the Watkins boy. He had spent a lot of time in the sloppy rented house where the Watkinses lived. The friendship had affected his manners and his neatness. Then he had begun to take some meals with the Watkinses, and to spend Saturday nights there. When he had moved most of his possessions over to the Watkinses' and had begun to spend more than half his nights there, Blake had been forced to act. He had spoken not to Charlie but to Mr. Watkins, and had, of necessity, said a number of things that must have sounded critical. Mr. Watkins' long and dirty hair and his corduroy jacket reassured Blake that he had been in the right.

But Mrs. Compton's dying smile and Mr. Watkins' dirty hair did not lessen the pleasure Blake took in setting himself in an uncomfortable seat on the five-forty-eight deep underground. The coach was old and smelled oddly like a bomb shelter in which whole families had spent the night. The light that spread from the ceiling down onto their heads and shoulders was dim. The filth on the window glass was streaked with rain from some other journey, and clouds of rank pipe and cigarette smoke had begun to rise from behind each newspaper, but it was a scene that meant to Blake that he was on a safe path, and after his brush with danger he even felt a little warmth toward Mrs. Compton and Mr. Watkins.

The train traveled up from underground into the weak daylight, and the slums and the city reminded Blake vaguely of the woman who had followed him. To avoid speculation or remorse about her, he turned his attention to the evening paper. Out of the corner of his eye he could see the landscape. It was industrial and, at that hour, sad. There were machine sheds and warehouses, and above these he saw a break in the clouds—a piece of yellow light. "Mr. Blake," someone said. He looked up. It was she. She was standing there holding one hand on the back of the seat to steady herself in the swaying coach. He remembered her name then—Miss Dent. "Hello, Miss Dent," he said.

"Do you mind if I sit here?"

"I guess not."

"Thank you. It's very kind of you. I don't like to inconvenience you like this. I don't want to..." He had been frightened when he looked up and saw her, but her timid voice rapidly reassured him. He shifted his hams—that futile and reflexive gesture of hospitality—and she sat down. She sighed. He smelled her wet clothing. She wore a formless black hat with a cheap crest stitched onto it. Her coat was thin cloth, he saw, and she wore gloves and carried a large pocketbook.

"Are you living out in this direction now, Miss Dent?"

"No."

She opened her purse and reached for her handkerchief. She had begun to cry. He turned his head to see if anyone in the car was looking, but no one was. He had sat beside a thousand passengers on the evening train. He had noticed their clothes, the holes in their gloves; and if they fell asleep and mumbled he had wondered what their worries were. He had classified almost all of them briefly before he buried his nose in the paper. He had marked them as rich, poor, brilliant or dull, neighbors or strangers, but no one of the thousand had ever wept. When she opened her purse, he remembered her perfume. It had clung to his skin the night he went to her place for a drink.

"I've been very sick," she said. "This is the first time I've been out of bed in two weeks. I've been terribly sick."

"I'm sorry that you've been sick, Miss Dent," he said in a voice loud enough to be heard by Mr. Watkins and Mrs. Compton. "Where are you working now?"

"What?"

"Where are you working now?"

"Oh, don't make me laugh," she said softly.

"I don't understand."

"You poisoned their minds."

He straightened his neck and braced his shoulders. These wrenching movements expressed a brief—and hopeless—longing to be in some other place. She meant trouble. He took a breath. He looked with deep feeling at the half-filled, half-lighted coach to affirm his sense of actuality, of a world in which there was not very much bad trouble after all. He was conscious of her heavy breathing and the smell of her rain-soaked coat. The train stopped. A nun and a man in overalls got off. When it started again, Blake put on his hat and reached for his raincoat.

"Where are you going?" she said.

"I'm going to the next car."

"Oh, no," she said. "No, no, no." She put her white face so close to his ear that he could feel her warm breath on his cheek. "Don't do that," she whispered. "Don't try and escape me. I have a pistol and I'll have to kill you and I don't want to. All I want to do is to talk with you. Don't move or I'll kill you. Don't, don't, don't!"

Blake sat back abruptly in his seat. If he had wanted to stand and shout for help, he would not have been able to. His tongue had swelled to twice its size, and when he tried to move it, it stuck horribly to the roof of his mouth. His legs were limp. All he could think of to do then was to wait for his heart to stop its hysterical beating, so that he could judge the extent of his danger. She was sitting a little sidewise, and in her pocketbook was the pistol, aimed at his belly.

"You understand me now, don't you?" she said. "You understand that I'm serious?" He tried to speak but he was still mute. He nodded his head. "Now we'll sit quietly for a little while," she said. "I got so excited that my thoughts are all confused. We'll sit quietly for a little while, until I can get my thoughts in order again."

Help would come, Blake thought. It was only a question of minutes. Someone, noticing the look on his face or her peculiar posture, would stop and interfere, and it would all be over. All he had to do was to wait until someone noticed his predicament. Out of the window he saw the river and the sky. The rain clouds were rolling down like a shutter, and while he watched, a streak of orange light on the horizon became brilliant. Its brilliance spread—he could see it move—across the waves until it raked the banks of the river with a dim firelight. Then it was put out. Help would come in a minute, he thought. Help would come before they stopped again; but the train stopped, there were some comings and goings, and Blake still lived on, at the mercy of the woman beside him. The possibility that help might not come was one that he could not face. The possibility that his predicament was not noticeable, that Mrs. Compton would guess that he was taking a poor relation out to dinner at Shady Hill, was something he would think about later. Then the saliva came back into his mouth and he was able to speak.

"Miss Dent?"

"Yes."

"What do you want?"

"I want to talk to you."

"You can come to my office."

"Oh, no. I went there every day for two weeks."

"You could make an appointment."

"No," she said. "I think we can talk here. I wrote you a letter but I've been too sick to go out and mail it. I've put down all my thoughts. I like to travel. I like trains. One of my troubles has always been that I could never afford to travel. I suppose you see this scenery every night and don't notice it any more, but it's nice for someone who's been in bed a long time. They say that He's not in the river and the hills but I think He is. 'Where shall wisdom be found?' it says. 'Where is the place of understanding? The depth saith it is not in me; the sea saith it is not with me. Destruction and death say we have heard the force with our ears.'

"Oh, I know what you're thinking," she said. "You're thinking that I'm crazy, and I have been very sick again but I'm going to be better. It's going to make me better to talk with you. I was in the hospital all the time before I came to work for you but they never tried to cure me, they only wanted to take away my self-respect. I haven't had any work now for three months. Even if I did have to kill you, they wouldn't be able to do anything to me except put me back in the hospital, so you see I'm not afraid. But let's sit quietly for a little while longer. I have to be calm."

The train continued its halting progress up the bank of the river, and Blake tried to force himself to make some plans for escape, but the immediate threat to his life made this difficult, and instead of planning sensibly, he thought of the many ways in which he could have avoided her in the first place. As soon as he had felt these regrets, he realized their futility. It was like regretting his lack of suspicion when she first mentioned her months in the hospital. It was like regretting his failure to have been warned by her shyness, her diffidence, and the handwriting that looked like the marks of a claw. There was no way of rectifying his mistakes, and he felt—for perhaps the first time in his mature life—the full force of regret. Out of the window, he saw some men fishing on the nearly dark river, and then a ramshackle boat club that seemed to have been nailed together out of scraps of wood that had been washed up on the shore.

Mr. Watkins had fallen asleep. He was snoring. Mrs. Compton read her paper. The train creaked, slowed, and halted infirmly at another station. Blake could see the southbound platform, where a few passengers were waiting to go into the city. There was a workman with a lunch pail, a dressed-up woman, and a woman with a suitcase. They stood apart from one another. Some advertisements were posted on the wall behind them. There was a picture of a couple drinking a toast in wine, a picture of a Cat's Paw rubber heel, and a picture of a Hawaiian dancer. Their cheerful intent seemed to go no farther than the puddles of water on the platform and to expire there. The platform and the people on it looked lonely. The train drew away from the station into the scattered lights of a slum and then into the darkness of the country and the river.

"I want you to read my letter before we get to Shady Hill," she said. "It's on the seat. Pick it up. I would have mailed it to you, but I've been too sick to go out. I haven't gone out for two weeks. I haven't had any work for three months. I haven't spoken to anybody but the landlady. Please read my letter."

He picked up the letter from the seat where she had put it. The cheap paper felt abhorrent and filthy to his fingers. It was folded and refolded. "Dear Husband," she had written, in that crazy, wandering hand, "they say that human love leads us to divine love, but is this true? I dream about you every night. I have such terrible desires. I have always had a gift for dreams. I dreamed on Tuesday of a volcano erupting with blood. When I was in the hospital they said they wanted to cure me but they only wanted to take away my self-respect. They only wanted me to dream about sewing and basket-work but I protected my gift for dreams. I'm clairvoyant. I can tell when the telephone is going to ring. I've never had a true friend in my whole life…."

The train stopped again. There was another platform, another picture of the couple drinking a toast, the rubber heel, and the Hawaiian dancer. Suddenly she pressed her face close to Blake's again and whispered in his ear. "I know what you're thinking. I can see it in your face. You're thinking you can get away from me in Shady Hill, aren't you? Oh, I've been planning this for weeks. It's all I've had to think about. I won't harm you if you'll let me talk. I've been thinking about devils. I mean, if there are devils in the world, if there are people in the world who represent evil, is it our duty to exterminate them? I know that you always prey on weak people. I can tell. Oh, sometimes I think I ought to kill you. Sometimes I think you're the only obstacle between me and my happiness. Sometimes…"

She touched Blake with the pistol. He felt the muzzle against his belly. The bullet, at that distance, would make a small hole where it entered, but it would rip out of his back a place as big as a soccer ball. He remembered the unburied dead he had seen in the war. The memory came in a rush; entrails, eyes, shattered bone, ordure, and other filth.

"All I've ever wanted in life is a little love," she said. She lightened the pressure of the gun. Mr. Watkins still slept. Mrs. Compton was sitting calmly with her hands folded in her lap. The coach rocked gently, and the coats and mushroom-colored raincoats that hung between the windows swayed a little as the car moved. Blake's elbow was on the window sill and his left shoe was on the guard above the steampipe. The car smelled like some dismal classroom. The passengers seemed asleep and apart, and Blake felt that he might never escape the smell of heat and wet clothing and the dimness of the light. He tried to summon the calculated self-deceptions with which he sometimes cheered himself, but he was left without any energy for hope of self-deception.

The conductor put his head in the door and said, "Shady Hill, next, Shady Hill."

"Now," she said. "Now you get out ahead of me."

Mr. Watkins waked suddenly, put on his coat and hat, and smiled at Mrs. Compton, who was gathering her parcels to her in a series of maternal gestures. They went to the door. Blake joined them, but neither of them spoke to him or seemed to notice the woman at his back. The conductor threw open the door, and Blake saw on the platform of the next car a few other neighbors who had missed the express, waiting patiently and tiredly in the wan light for their trip to the end. He raised his head to see through the open door the abandoned mansion out of town, a NO TRESPASSING sign nailed to a tree, and then the oil tanks. The concrete abutments of the bridge passed, so close to the open door that he could have touched them. Then he saw the first of the lampposts on the northbound platform, the sign SHADY HILL in black and gold, and the little lawn and flower bed kept up by the Improvement Association, and then the cab stand and a corner of the old-fashioned depot. It was raining again; it was pouring. He could hear the splash of water and see the lights reflected in puddles and in the shining pavement, and the idle sound of splashing and dripping formed in his mind a conception of shelter, so light and strange that it seemed to belong to a time of his life that he could not remember.

He went down the steps with her at his back. A dozen or so cars were waiting by the station with their motors running. A few people got off from each of the other coaches; he recognized most of them, but none of them offered to give him a ride. They walked separately or in pairs—purposefully out of the rain to the shelter of the platform, where the car horns called to them. It was time to go home, time for a drink, time for love, time for supper, and he could see the lights on the hill—lights by which children were being bathed, meat cooked, dishes washed—shining in the rain. One by one, the cars picked up the heads of families, until there were only four left. Two of the stranded passengers drove off in the only taxi the village had. "I'm sorry, darling," a woman said tenderly to her husband when she drove up a few minutes later. "All our clocks are slow." The last man looked at his watch, looked at the rain, and then walked off into it, and Blake saw him go as if they had some reason to say goodbye—not as we say goodbye to friends after a party but as we say goodbye when we are faced with an inexorable and unwanted parting of the spirit and the heart. The man's footsteps sounded as he crossed the parking lot to the sidewalk, and then they were lost. In the station, a telephone began to ring. The ringing was loud, evenly spaced, and unanswered. Someone wanted to know about the next train to Albany, but Mr. Flanagan, the stationmaster, had gone home an hour ago. He had turned on all his lights before he went away. They burned in the empty waiting room. They burned, tin-shaded, at intervals up and down the platform and with the peculiar sadness of dim and purposeless lights. They lighted the Hawaiian dancer, the couple drinking a toast, the rubber heel.

"I've never been here before," she said. "I thought it would look different. I didn't think it would look so shabby. Let's get out of the light. Go over there."

His legs felt sore. All his strength was gone. "Go on," she said.

North of the station there were a freight house and a coalyard and an inlet where the butcher and the baker and the man who ran the service station moored the dinghies, from which they fished on Sundays, sunk now to the gunwales with the rain. As he walked toward the freight house, he saw a movement on the ground and heard a scraping sound, and then he saw a rat take its head out of a paper bag and regard him. The rat seized the bag in its teeth and dragged it into a culvert.

"Stop," she said. "Turn around. Oh, I ought to feel sorry for you. Look at your poor face. But you don't know what I've been through. I'm afraid to go out in the daylight. I'm afraid the blue sky will fall down on me. I'm like poor Chicken-Licken. I only feel like myself when it begins to get dark. But still and all I'm better than you. I still have good dreams sometimes. I dream about picnics and heaven and the brotherhood of man, and about castles in the moonlight and a river with willow trees all along the edge of it and foreign cities, and after all I know more about love than you."

He heard from off the dark river the drone of an outboard motor, a sound that drew slowly behind it across the dark water such a burden of clear, sweet memories of gone summers and gone pleasures that it made his flesh crawl, and he thought of dark in the mountains and the children singing. "They never wanted to cure me," she said. "They…" The noise of a train coming down from the north drowned out her voice, but she went on talking. The noise filled his ears, and the windows where people ate drank, slept, and read flew past. When the train had passed beyond the bridge, the noise grew distant, and he heard her screaming at him, *"Kneel down! Kneel down! Do what I say. Kneel down!"*

He got to his knees. He bent his head. "There," she said. "You see, if you do what I say, I won't harm you, because I really don't want to harm you, I want to help you, but when I see your face it sometimes seems to me that I can't help you. Sometimes it seems to me that if I were good and loving and sane—oh, much better than I am—sometimes it seems to me that if I were all these things and young and beautiful, too, and if I called to show you the right way, you wouldn't heed me. Oh, I'm better than you, I'm better than you, and I shouldn't waste my time or spoil my life like this. Put your face in the dirt. *Put your face in the dirt!* Do what I say. Put your face in the dirt."

He fell forward in the filth. The coal skinned his face. He stretched out on the ground, weeping. "Now I feel better," she said. "Now I can wash my hands of you, I can wash my hands of all this, because you see there is some kindness, some saneness in me that I can find and use. I can wash my hands." Then he heard her footsteps go away from him, over the rubble. He heard the clearer and more distant sound they made on the hard surface of the platform. He heard them diminish. He raised his head. He saw her climb the stairs of the wooden footbridge and cross it and go down to the other platform, where her figure in the dim light looked small, common, and harmless. He raised himself out of the dust—warily at first, until he saw by her attitude, her looks, that she had forgotten him; that she had completed what she had wanted to do, and that he was safe. He got to his feet and picked up his hat from the ground where it had fallen and walked home.

Guides to Reflection

1. A Flannery O'Connor short story will typically show a well-defended character barricaded within his own habits and then bring his world into harsh contact with reality. The result is a breakdown that sometimes leads to a breakthrough. How is Blake presented to us in "The Five-Forty-Eight"? What constitutes his world? What happens to him when under attack?

2. Miss Dent is introduced in the opening lines as someone who has "loathing and purpose" written all over her face. She remains in hot pursuit over the course of the story until in the end she "gets her man." Cheever initially emphasizes her vulnerability, reveals her mental and emotional disturbance, but shows her quite masterfully taking control at the end. Finally powerful, and with Blake in the dirt at her feet, she is able to show him mercy and then "wash her hands" of the whole business. Is what happens to her in the course of the story a breakdown or a breakthrough for her?

3. When Blake feels the muzzle of the woman's gun in his belly, he remembers the unburied dead he had seen in the war. "The memory came in a rush: entrails, eyes, shattered bone, ordure, and other filth" *(Reader, 20)*. What might this flashback explain about his character?

4. Cheever introduces into this story verses 12, 14, and 22 from the 28th chapter of the book of Job *(Reader, 19)*. Is the presence of Scripture here only the raving of a disturbed woman who fancies herself an avenging angel or does the biblical text have a larger, more positive significance?

5. The parable of the prodigal son (Luke 15) ends at a standstill, without the elder brother making a response to the father's words of affirmation and explanation. The reader does not know what will happen next. Cheever uses a similar technique here. What do you think Blake will be when he rises up from the dust and returns home? Does the story hint at this, or is the reader left with his or her own choices to make?

2

Mary Gordon

Early in her career, Mary Gordon was asked about famous contemporary writers who shun telling stories of people's lives and instead construct self-enclosed worlds of word play in their novels. Gordon responded: "Let them do it as long as I don't ever have to read it. I just find it totally boring.... I don't particularly like the... trip where literature is about literature.... I think novels should be about people."[1] Mary Gordon's work—her novels, short stories, essays, and memoir—have all focused on people, particularly on the decisions they must make about other people and things important to them: parents, children, work, money, love, death, and—for many of her characters—religion.

Because the protagonists in Gordon's first novels, *Final Payments* (1978) and *The Company of Women* (1980), seek to define their childhood relationships to the Roman Catholic Church, Gordon was quickly labeled a "Catholic writer" by critics. While Gordon finds this label "too limiting,"[2] she has frequently spoken and written about the importance of Catholicism to her life and her art. In her essay "Getting Here from There," Gordon describes her family's religious life, saying "my childhood days were shaped and marked by the religious devotions of my parents, by the rhythmic, repetitive cadences of formal prayer."[3] Of her parents, Gordon says, "... both of them could say with truthfulness that their faith was the most important thing in the world to them."[4] Gordon's father regularly took her to worship and taught her the Latin mass when she was five. The church's stories of heroic women who became saints appealed to Gordon, and she aspired to become a nun. In grade school she wrote treatises on subjects such as prayer and the Trinity.[5]

The religious legacy Gordon's parents gave her was complex, as were other aspects of their lives. Gordon's mother, the child of Irish and Italian immigrants, grew up in the ethnic, working-class neighborhood on New York's Long Island where Gordon herself grew up. Gordon's father, born a Jew in Lithuania, converted to Catholicism as an adult in the 1930s. Gordon has said that his was an "intellectual conversion," spurred by the fact that "he supported Franco," the right-wing Spanish dictator.[6] Throughout his life,

Gordon's father espoused right-wing political ideas and anti-Semitic views as well, positions Gordon herself finds untenable and disturbing. Gordon's knowledge of her father's life and beliefs is complicated, both because he died when she was seven and, she has discovered recently, he misled her and her mother about the half-century of his life before he met and married Gordon's mother. In her memoir-biography *Shadow Man* (1996), Gordon describes her shock at discovering that stories she had treasured of her father's life, such as his studies at Harvard and travels as a young man in Europe, were untrue. In fact, he was a high school dropout from Lorain, Ohio, who moved from job to job, never finding success at anything for long. Gordon surmises he must have continued to read and study on his own after he left high school because he knew seven or eight languages and, during Gordon's childhood, wrote articles for various journals in New York. Whatever the truth about the first 50 years of his life, his intellectual and spiritual influence on Gordon was profound. As a father, he dedicated himself to educating Gordon and nurturing her faith. His intense devotion to her is captured in a statement Gordon remembers him making to her: "I love you more than God."[7]

Asked in interviews about her own beliefs and her views on the Roman Catholic Church, Gordon's responses indicate they are dynamic and complex. Critical of the church's treatment of women and teachings about sexuality, Gordon also laments the "unlovely" liturgies that characterize much contemporary worship.[8] Recently she has written about her own participation in religious services and the religious questions raised by her mother's decline into senility.[9] While she notes that Catholicism has been a "template"[10] for her work, Gordon has been careful to distinguish between holding particular beliefs, and writing about characters who hold various beliefs or none at all. She rigorously distinguishes art from religion, asserting that "All beauty is not religious in its nature, and all aesthetic or heartfelt responses are not religious.... If you call everything religious, then nothing is religious."[11] Gordon differentiates between art and religion in this way:

> To my mind, an experience to be properly religious must include three things: an ethical component, the possibility of full participation by the entire human community, and acknowledgment of the existence of a life beyond the human. Art need do none of these things, although it may.[12]

Particularly striking in Gordon's treatment of religion in her fiction are the presence of clear religious concerns and the variety of beliefs her characters hold. Their beliefs, devotion, and practices reflect the religious diversity present in contemporary America.

While Gordon is best known for her five novels, the most recent being *Spending: A Utopian Divertimento* (1998), she has also written three novellas and many short stories, 20 of which appear in the collection *Temporary Shelter* (1987). The last story in the collection, "Mrs. Cassidy's Last Year," tells of an elderly man's struggle to keep a promise to his senile wife. Mr. Cassidy's religious faith seems to aid him as he cares for his wife, seeking to assure that she will die in her own bed as he had vowed early in their marriage she would. He attends mass, prays, and hopes for forgiveness from his family for past failures. When in a moment of anger he wishes his wife dead, he refuses to break the promise he made to her, seeing it as an extension of his marriage vow. Although Mr. Cassidy himself will not receive communion because he "had sinned against charity,"[13] he looks compassionately on the others who do not go to receive it, thinking their sins were not serious enough to warrant staying back. Mr. Cassidy's generosity is mirrored in the ritual of the Mass. The priest begins the service with arms open in welcome. At the conclusion of the Mass he blesses the congregation. The priest, who offers encouragement to Mr. Cassidy, embodies the comfort and respite the church offers. More difficult to assess in the story is God. Mrs. Cassidy's condition and Mr. Cassidy's faith raise age-old questions: Where is God when people suffer? Why does a loving God allow such sorrow, such decay? Does God even hear the prayers of those who suffer? In "Mrs. Cassidy's Last Year," the church may not fully explain the mystery of God's ways, but it provides a shelter for Mr. Cassidy as he struggles to remain faithful to his promises and beliefs, and as he strives to love and serve his dying wife.

Paula J. Carlson

Notes

1. Diana Cooper-Clark, "An Interview with Mary Gordon," *Commonweal* (9 May 1980): 272.

2. Alma Bennett, "Conversations with Mary Gordon," *South Carolina Review* 28 (Fall, 1995): 33.

3. Mary Gordon, "Getting Here from There: A Writer's Reflections on a Religious Past," in *Good Boys and Dead Girls and Other Essays* (New York: Penguin, 1991), 161.

4. Ibid., 166.

5. Bennett, 25.

6. Patrick H. Samway, "An Interview with Mary Gordon," *America* 170, no. 17 (14 May 1994): 12.

7. Mary Gordon, *Shadow Man* (New York: Vintage, 1997), XVIII.

8. "Getting Here," 175.

9. "Still Life," *Harper's* 297, no. 1783 (Dec. 1998): 48-53.

10. Bennett, 24.

11. Cooper-Clark, 270.

12. "Getting Here," 173.

13. Mary Gordon, "Mrs. Cassidy's Last Year," in *Temporary Shelter* (New York: Random House, 1987), 197.

Mrs. Cassidy's Last Year

Mr. Cassidy knew he couldn't go to Communion. He had sinned against charity. He had wanted his wife dead.

The intention had been his, and the desire. She would not go back to bed. She had lifted the table that held her breakfast (it was unfair, it was unfair to all of them, that the old woman should be so strong, and so immobile). She had lifted the table above her head and sent it crashing to the floor in front of him.

"Rose," he had said, bending, wondering how he would get scrambled egg, coffee, cranberry juice (which she had said she liked, the color of it) out of the garden pattern on the carpet. That was the sort of thing she knew but would not tell him now. She would laugh, wicked and bland-faced as an egg, when he did the wrong thing. But never say what was right, although she knew it, and her tongue was not dead for curses, for reports of crimes.

"Shithawk," she would shout at him from her bedroom. "Bastard son of a whore." Or more mildly, "Pimp," or "Fathead fart."

Old words, curses heard from soldiers on the boat or somebody's street children. Never spoken by her until now. Punishing him, though he had kept his promise.

He was trying to pick up the scrambled eggs with a paper napkin. The napkin broke, then shredded when he tried to squeeze the egg into what was left of it. He was on his knees on the carpet, scraping egg, white shreds of paper, purple fuzz from the trees in the carpet.

"Shitscraper," she laughed at him on his knees.

And then he wished in his heart most purely for the woman to be dead.

The doorbell rang. His son and his son's wife. Shame that they should see him so, kneeling, hearing curses, cursing in his heart.

"Pa," said Toni, kneeling next to him. "You see what we mean."

"She's too much for you," said Mr. Cassidy's son Tom. Self-made man, thought Mr. Cassidy. Good time Charlie. Every joke a punchline like a whip.

No one would say his wife was too much for him.

"Swear," she had said, lying next to him in bed when they were each no more than thirty. Her eyes were wild then. What had made her think of it? No sickness near them, and fearful age some continent like Africa, with no one they knew well. What had put the thought to her, and the wildness, so that her nails bit into his palm, as if she knew small pain would preserve his memory.

"Swear you will let me die in my own bed. Swear you won't let them take me away."

He swore, her nails making dents in his palms, a dull shallow pain, not sharp, blue-green or purplish.

He had sworn.

On his knees now beside his daughter-in-law, his son.

"She is not too much for me. She is my wife."

"Leave him then, Toni," said Tom. "Let him do it himself if it's so god-damn easy. Serve him right. Let him learn the hard way. He couldn't do it if he didn't have us, the slobs around the corner."

Years of hatred now come out, punishing for not being loved best, of the family's children not most prized. Nothing is forgiven, thought the old man, rising to his feet, his hand on his daughter-in-law's squarish shoulder.

He knelt before the altar of God. The young priest, bright-haired, faced them, arms open, a good little son.

No sons priests. He thought how he was old enough now to have a priest a grandson. This boy before him, vested and ordained, could have been one of the ones who followed behind holding tools. When there was time. He thought of Tom looking down at his father who knelt trying to pick up food. Tom for whom there had been no time. Families were this: the bulk, the knot of memory, wounds remembered not only because they had set on the soft, the pliable wax of childhood, motherhood, fatherhood, closeness to death. Wounds most deeply set and best remembered because families are days, the sameness of days and words, hammer blows, smothering, breath grabbed, memory on the soft skull, in the lungs, not once only but again and again the same. The words and the starvation.

Tom would not forget, would not forgive him. Children thought themselves the only wounded.

Should we let ourselves in for it, year after year, he asked in prayer, believing God did not hear him.

Tom would not forgive him for being the man he was. A man who paid debts, kept promises. Mr. Cassidy knelt up straighter, proud of himself before God.

Because of the way he had to be. He knelt back again, not proud. As much sense to be proud of the color of his hair. As much choice.

It was his wife who was the proud one. As if she thought it could have been some other way. The house, the children. He knew, being who they were they must have a house like that, children like that. Being who they were to the world. Having their faces.

As if she thought with some wrong turning these things might have been wasted. Herself a slattern, him drunk, them living in a tin shack, children dead or missing.

One was dead. John, the favorite, lost somewhere in a plane. The war dead. There was his name on the plaque near the altar. With the other town boys. And she had never forgiven him. For what he did not know. For helping bring that child into the world? Better, she said, to have borne none than the pain of losing this one, the most beautiful, the bravest. She turned from him then, letting some shelf drop, like a merchant at the hour of closing. And Tom had not forgotten the grief at his brother's death, knowing he could not have closed his mother's heart like that.

Mr. Cassidy saw they were all so unhappy, hated each other so because they thought things could be different. As he had thought of his wife. He had imagined she could be different if she wanted to. Which had angered him. Which was not, was almost never, the truth about things.

Things were as they were going to be, he thought, watching the boy-faced priest giving out Communion. Who were the others not receiving? Teenagers, pimpled, believing themselves in sin. He wanted to tell them they were not. He was sure they were not. Mothers with babies. Not going to Communion because they took the pill, it must be. He thought they should not stay away, although he thought they should not do what they had been told not to. He knew that the others in their seats were there for the heat of their bodies. While he sat back for the coldness of his heart, a heart that had wished his wife dead. He had wished the one dead he had promised he would love forever.

The boy priest blessed the congregation. Including Mr. Cassidy himself.

"Pa," said Tom, walking beside his father, opening the car door for him. "You see what we mean about her?"

"It was my fault. I forgot."

"Forgot what?" said Tom, emptying his car ashtray onto the church parking lot. Not my son, thought Mr. Cassidy, turning his head.

"How she is," said Mr. Cassidy. "I lost my temper."

"Pa, you're not God," said Tom. His hands were on the steering wheel, angry. His mother's.

"Okay," said Toni. "But look, Pa, you've been a saint to her. But she's not the woman she was. Not the woman we knew."

She's the woman I married."

"Not any more," said Toni, wife of her husband.

If not, then who? People were the same. They kept their bodies. They did not become someone else. Rose was the woman he had married, a green girl, high-colored, with beautifully cut nostrils, hair that fell down always, hair she pinned up swiftly, with anger. She had been a housemaid and he a chauffeur. He had taken her to the ocean. They wore straw hats. They were not different people now. She was the girl he had seen first, the woman he had married, the mother of his children, the woman he had promised: Don't let them take me. Let me die in my own bed.

"Supposing it was yourself and Tom, then, Toni," said Mr. Cassidy, remembering himself a gentleman. "What would you want him to do? Would you want him to break his promise?"

"I hope I'd never make him promise anything like that," said Toni.

"But if you did?"

"I don't believe in those kinds of promises."

"My father thinks he's God. You have to understand. There's no two ways about anything."

For what was his son now refusing to forgive him? He was silent now, sitting in the back of the car. He looked at the top of his daughter-in-law's head, blond now, like some kind of circus candy. She had never been blond. Why did they do it? Try to be what they were not born to. Rose did not.

"What I wish you'd get through your head, Pa, is that it's me and Toni carrying the load. I suppose you forget where all the suppers come from?"

"I don't forget."

"Why don't you think of Toni for once?"

"I think of her, Tom, and you too. I know what you do. I'm very grateful. Mom is grateful, too, or she would be."

But first I think of my wife to whom I made vows. And whom I promised.

"The doctor thinks you're nuts, you know that, don't you?" said Tom. "Rafferty thinks you're nuts to try and keep her. He thinks we're nuts to go along with you. He says he washes his hands of the whole bunch of us."

The doctor washes his hands, thought Mr. Cassidy, seeing Leo Rafferty, hale as a dog, at his office sink.

The important thing was not to forget she was the woman he had married.

So he could leave the house, so he could leave her alone, he strapped her into the bed. Her curses were worst when he released her. She had grown a beard this last year, like a goat.

Like a man?

No.

He remembered her as she was when she was first his wife. A white night-gown, then as now. So she was the same. He'd been told it smelled different a virgin's first time. And never that way again. Some blood. Not much. As if she hadn't minded.

He sat her in the chair in front of the television. They had Mass now on television for sick people, people like her. She pushed the button on the little box that could change channels from across the room. One of their grandsons was a TV repairman. He had done it for them when she got sick. She pushed the button to a station that showed cartoons. Mice in capes, cats outraged. Some stories now with colored children. He boiled an egg for her lunch.

She sat chewing, looking at the television. What was that look in her eyes now? Why did he want to call it wickedness? Because it was blank and hate-ful. Because there was no light. Eyes should have light. There should be something behind them. That was dangerous, nothing behind her eyes but hate. Sullen like a bull kept from a cow. Sex mad. Why did that look make him think of sex? Sometimes he was afraid she wanted it.

He did not know what he would do.

She slept. He slept in the chair across from her.

The clock went off for her medicine. He got up from the chair, gauging the weather. Sometimes the sky was green this time of year. It was warm when it should not be. He didn't like that. The mixup made him shaky. It made him say to himself, "Now I am old."

He brought her the medicine. Three pills, red and grey, red and yellow, dark pink. Two just to keep her quiet. Sometimes she sucked them and spat them out when they melted and she got the bad taste. She thought they were candy. It was their fault for making them those colors. But it was something else he had to think about. He had to make sure she swallowed them right away.

Today she was not going to swallow. He could see that by the way her eyes looked at the television. The way she set her mouth so he could see what she had done with the pills, kept them in a pocket in her cheek, as if for storage.

"Rose," he said, stepping between her and the television, breaking her gaze. "You've got to swallow the pills. They cost money."

She tried to look over his shoulder. On the screen an ostrich, dressed in colored stockings, danced down the road. He could see she was not listening to him. And he tried to remember what the young priest had said when he came to bring Communion, what his daughter June had said. Be patient with her. Humor her. She can't help what she does. She's not the woman she once was.

She is the same.

"Hey, my Rose, won't you just swallow the pills for me. Like my girl."

She pushed him out of the way. So she could go on watching the television. He knelt down next to her.

"Come on, girleen. It's the pills make you better."

She gazed over the top of his head. He stood up, remembering what was done to animals.

He stroked her throat as he had stroked the throats of dogs and horses, a boy on a farm. He stroked the old woman's loose, papery throat, and said, "Swallow, then, just swallow."

She looked over his shoulder at the television. She kept the pills in a corner of her mouth.

It was making him angry. He put one finger above her lip under her nose and one below her chin, so that she would not be able to open her mouth. She breathed through her nose like a patient animal. She went on looking at the television. She did not swallow.

"You swallow them, Rose, this instant," he said, clamping her mouth shut. "They cost money. The doctor says you must. You're throwing good money down the drain."

Now she was watching a lion and a polar bear dancing. There were pianos in their cages.

He knew he must move away or his anger would make him do something. He had promised he would not be angry. He would remember who she was.

He went into the kitchen with a new idea. He would give her something sweet that would make her want to swallow. There was ice cream in the refrigerator. Strawberry that she liked. He removed each strawberry and placed it in the sink so she would not chew and then get the taste of the medicine. And then spit it out, leaving him, leaving them both no better than when they began.

He brought the dish of ice cream to her in the living room. She was sitting staring at the television with her mouth open. Perhaps she had opened her mouth to laugh? At what? At what was this grown woman laughing? A zebra was playing a xylophone while his zebra wife hung striped pajamas on a line.

In opening her mouth, she had let the pills fall together onto her lap. He saw the three of them, wet, stuck together, at the center of her lap. He thought he would take the pills and simply hide them in the ice cream. He bent to fish them from the valley of her lap.

And then she screamed at him. And then she stood up.

He was astonished at her power. She had not stood by herself for seven months. She put one arm in front of her breasts and raised the other against him, knocking him heavily to the floor.

"No," she shouted, her voice younger, stronger, the voice of a well young man. "Don't think you can have it now. That's what you're after. That's what you're always after. You want to get into it. I'm not one of your whores. You always thought it was such a great prize. I wish you'd have it cut off. I'd like to cut it off."

And she walked out of the house. He could see her wandering up and down the street in the darkness.

He dragged himself over to the chair and propped himself against it so he could watch her through the window. But he knew he could not move any farther. His leg was light and foolish underneath him, and burning with pain. He could not move any more, not even to the telephone that was half a yard away from him. He could see her body, visible through her nightgown, as she walked the street in front of the house.

He wondered if he should call out or be silent. He did not know how far she would walk. He could imagine her walking until the land stopped, and then into the water. He could not stop her. He would not raise his voice.

There was that pain in his leg that absorbed him strangely, as if it were the pain of someone else. He knew the leg was broken. "I have broken my leg," he kept saying to himself, trying to connect the words and the burning.

But then he remembered what it meant. He would not be able to walk. He would not be able to take care of her.

"Rose," he shouted, trying to move toward the window.

And then, knowing he could not move and she could not hear him, "Help."

He could see the green numbers on the clock, alive as cat's eyes. He could see his wife walking in the middle of the street. At least she was not walking far. But no one was coming to help her.

He would have to call for help. And he knew what it meant: they would take her away somewhere. No one would take care of her in the house if he did not. And he could not move.

No one could hear him shouting. No one but he could see his wife, wandering up and down the street in her nightgown.

They would take her away. He could see it; he could hear the noises. Policemen in blue, car radios reporting other disasters, young boys writing his words down in notebooks. And doctors, white coats, white shoes, wheeling her out. Her strapped. She would curse him. She would curse him rightly for having broken his promise. And the young men would wheel her out. Almost everyone was younger than he now. And he could hear how she would be as they wheeled her past him, rightly cursing.

Now he could see her weaving in the middle of the street. He heard a car slam on its brakes to avoid her. He thought someone would have to stop then. But he heard the car go on down to the corner.

No one could hear him shouting in the living room. The windows were shut; it was late October. There was a high bulk of grey cloud, showing islands of fierce, acidic blue. He would have to do something to get someone's attention before the sky became utterly dark and the drivers could not see her wandering before their cars. He could see her wandering; he could see the set of her angry back. She was wearing only her nightgown. He would have to get someone to bring her in before she died of cold.

The only objects he could reach were the figurines that covered the low table beside him. He picked one up: a bust of Robert Kennedy. He threw it through the window. The breaking glass made a violent, disgraceful noise. It was the sound of disaster he wanted. It must bring help.

He lay still for ten minutes, waiting, looking at the clock. He could see her walking, cursing. She could not hear him. He was afraid no one could hear him. He picked up another figurine, a bicentennial eagle and threw it through the window next to the one he had just broken. Then he picked up another and threw it through the window next to that. He went on: six windows. He went on until he had broken every window in the front of the house.

He had ruined his house. The one surprising thing of his long lifetime. The broken glass winked like green jewels, hard sea creatures, on the purple carpet. He looked at what he had destroyed. He would never have done it; it was something he would never have done. But he would not have believed he was a man who could not keep his promise.

In the dark he lay and prayed that someone would come and get her. That was the only thing now to pray for; the one thing he had asked God to keep back. A car stopped in front of the house. He heard his son's voice speaking to his mother. He could see the two of them; Tom had his arm around her. She was walking into the house now as if she had always meant to.

Mr. Cassidy lay back for the last moment of darkness. Soon the room would be full.

His son turned on the light.

Guides to Reflection

1. Although the entire story takes place on one day, we learn quite a bit about Mr. Cassidy and his relationships with his wife and children. What kind of person is Mr. Cassidy? What seem to be the emotionally crucial times of his life? How do those times affect his religious belief?

2. Over and over in the story, Mr. Cassidy asserts that his wife, Rose, is the same woman now in old age that she was when he married her. What evidence is there in the story to suggest the kind of person Rose was and is?

3. In an interview in 1988, Gordon made this statement about the church: "One of the things that is good about the church is it's a place for people to go who aren't winning in the world's terms to have a kind of shelter and a kind of place."[1] Comment on her view of the church here and her presentation of the church in "Mrs. Cassidy's Last Year."

4. Mr. Cassidy steadfastly holds to two things in the story: he insists on keeping his promise to Rose, and he maintains that much of the way we are is beyond our control. We are who we are and can actually change very little about our lives. Do you agree with Mr. Cassidy's positions on promises and fate? Why or why not?

Notes

1. M. Deiter Keyishian, "Radical Damage: An Interview with Mary Gordon," *The Literary Review* 32 (1988): 73.

3

Wendell Berry

Wendell Berry is, without apology, an anachronism. In an America increasingly suburban, on the move, and driven by the ideals of a global economy, he celebrates the virtue of staying put and digging deep. After a few years of study at Stanford and teaching in New York City, he returned in 1965 to Henry County, Kentucky, where his family had farmed since the early nineteenth century. Living now in Port Royal, only miles from that earliest homestead, he ploughs his land with horses, practices an organic agriculture advocated by the Rodale Press (his current employer), and gives voice in poetry, fiction, and essays to a largely vanished way of life.

Berry's entire enterprise, both the farming and the publishing, is energized by his conviction that human beings are profoundly connected to the world as creatures within a Creation. What distinguishes us in this divine order is our ability to "husband" the world as its stewards or, conversely, to divorce ourselves from it. In his writing Berry eulogizes our marriage to the physical world and, often with prophetic intensity, denounces the "great divorce" exemplified by shortsighted construction of highways and dams, strip mining, and agribusiness. He is in the most profound sense of the word an ecologist, aware that the damage we do to the land we also do to ourselves. For our own survival we must learn that what is good for the world is good for us, not the other way around: "We must abandon arrogance and stand in awe. We must recover the sense of the majesty of creation, and the ability to be worshipful in its presence."[1] To look at a stand of "great trees," therefore, should not present an opportunity for lumber or for tourism. Rather, the trees are "apostles of the living light," and to see them in multicolored autumn is to behold nothing less than the world's liturgy:

In fall their brightened leaves, released,
Fly down the wind, and we are pleased
To walk on radiance, amazed.
O light come down to earth, be praised![2]

Berry's language, in his prose writing as well as in his poetry, suggests how his vision is essentially religious. Worshipful, he stands in humility before the created world, "in which the Creator, the formative and quickening spirit, is still immanent and at work."³ Yet despite his markedly Christian frame of reference, he avoids the church in favor of the creation, keeping his Sabbath well outside any sanctuary walls. To quote Isaiah 14:7, the epitaph to his latest collection of poems, *A Timbered Choir* (1997), "The whole earth is at rest and quiet; they break forth into singing." Berry's antipathy is directed to that brand of Christianity that prizes heaven by neglecting (or even despising) the earth, that excerpts the Creator from the creation. "The Bible's aim, as I read it, is not the freeing of the spirit from the world. It is the handbook of their interaction. It says that they cannot be divided; that their mutuality, their unity, is inescapable." What else can be meant by the resurrection of the body, he asks, but the eternal harmony of spirit and matter?⁴

The interdependence of human beings and the land they live on, as well as the moral effect of "care and competence and frugality,"⁵ are hallmarks of Berry's fiction as well as his essays. His eight novels and collections of short stories, set in a fictional Port William that closely recalls his ancestral Port Royal, explore the lives of seven generations of farm families over the first half of the twentieth century. These intertwining narratives move back and forth in time over a single landscape of ridges, hollows, streams, and arable land. A few family names, the shared place where they are born and buried, all remain constant; but each successive story, like the five collected in *Fidelity* (1992), discovers the hint of a common origin and convergent destiny, and excavates a new depth of connection. As the narrator of "Pray without Ceasing" observes: "You work your way down, or not so much down as within, into the interior of the present, until finally you come to that beginning in which all things, the world and the light itself, at a word welled up into being out of their absence" *(Reader, 40)*.

"Pray without Ceasing" is an excavation of memory, in which an old woman's account of an untold family history makes the past present and reveals to the narrator that he is the child of his grandfather's forgiveness. The story reconstructs this identity by going back two generations, moving from 1990 to a Saturday morning in July 1912. We see how a concatenation of events leads blindly to a killing, how an instinctive desire for revenge is quite literally blocked from taking place, how forgiveness is the proper response to a common tragedy. Murder and suicide have their day in this story, but Berry surprises us with how little effect they come to have—not because of anyone's forgetfulness but, rather, because of one man's forgiveness. Berry helps us to see why the sins of the fathers need not be visited upon their children.

Peter S. Hawkins

Notes

1. Wendell Berry, "A Native Hill" in *Recollected Essays 1965–1980* (San Francisco: North Point Press, 1984), 98. For Berry's most stinging indictment of our destructive mishandling of the created order, see *The Unsettling of America: Culture and Agriculture* (San Francisco: Sierra Club Books, 1977).

2. "Sabbath, 1986," *A Timbered Choir: The Sabbath Poems 1979–1997* (Washington, DC: Counterpoint, 1998), 83. For discussions of Berry's particular blend of "spiritual and ecological awareness," see Andrew J. Angyal, *Wendell Berry* (New York: Twayne Publishers, 1995), 132-133 and Leonard M. Scigaj, *Sustainable Poetry: Four American Ecopoets* (Lexington, Ky.: University Press of Kentucky, 1999), 167-171.

3. Wendell Berry, "A Secular Pilgrimage" in *A Continuous Harmony: Essays Cultural and Agricultural* (New York: Harcourt Brace Jovanovich, Inc., 1972), 6. This essay, ostensibly about other nature poets, is clearly Berry's self-description. Another essay in this volume, "Discipline and Hope," makes a succinct, powerful statement of his philosophy.

4. Berry, "A Native Hill" in *A Continuous Harmony*, 284-285.

Pray without Ceasing

Mat Feltner was my grandfather on my mother's side. Saying it thus, I force myself to reckon again with the strangeness of that verb *was*. The man of whom I once was pleased to say, "He is my grandfather," has become the dead man who was my grandfather. He was, and is no more. And this is a part of the great mystery we call time.

But the past is present also. And this, I think, is a part of the greater mystery we call eternity. Though Mat Feltner has been dead for twenty-five years, and I am now older than he was when I was born and have grandchildren of my own, I know his hands, their way of holding a hammer or a hoe or a set of checklines, as well as I know my own. I know his way of talking, his way of cocking his head when he began a story, the smoking pipe stem held an inch from his lips. I have in my mind, not just as a memory but as a consolation, his welcome to me when I returned home from the university and, later, from jobs in distant cities. When I sat down beside him, his hand would clap lightly onto my leg above the knee; my absence might have lasted many months, but he would say as though we had been together the day before, "Hello, Andy." The shape of his hand is printed on the flesh of my thigh as vividly as a birthmark. This man who was my grandfather is present in me, as I felt always his father to be present in him. His father was Ben. The known history of the Feltners in Port William begins with Ben.

But even the unknown past is present in us, its silence as persistent as a ringing in the ears. When I stand in the road that passes through Port William, I am standing on the strata of my history that go down through the known past into the unknown: the blacktop rests on state gravel, which rests on county gravel, which rests on the creek rock and cinders laid down by the town when it was still mostly beyond the reach of the county; and under the creek rock and cinders is the dirt track of the town's beginning, the buffalo trace that was the way we came. You work your way down, or not so much down as within, into the interior of the present, until finally you come to that beginning in which all things, the world and the light itself, at a word welled up into being out of their absence. And nothing is here that we are beyond the reach of merely because we do not know about it. It is always the first morning of Creation and always the last day, always the now that is in time and the Now that is not, that has filled time with reminders of Itself.

When my grandfather was dying, I was not thinking about the past. My grandfather was still a man I knew, but as he subsided day by day he was ceasing to be the man I had known. I was experiencing consciously for the first time that transformation in which the living, by dying, pass into the living, and I was full of grief and love and wonder.

And so when I came out of the house one morning after breakfast and found Braymer Hardy sitting in his pickup truck in front of my barn, I wasn't expecting any news. Braymer was an old friend of my father's; he was curious to see what Flora and I would do with the long-abandoned Harford Place that we had bought and were fixing up, and sometimes he visited. His way was not to go to the door and knock. He just drove in and stopped his old truck at the barn and sat looking around until somebody showed up.

"Well, you ain't much of a Catlett," he said, in perfect good humor. "Marce Catlett would have been out and gone two hours ago."

"I do my chores *before* breakfast," I said, embarrassed by the lack of evidence. My grandfather Catlett would, in fact, have been out and gone two hours ago.

"But," Braymer said in an explanatory tone, as if talking to himself, "I reckon your daddy is a late sleeper, being as he's an office man. But that Wheeler was always a shotgun once he *got* out," he went on, clearly implying, and still in excellent humor, that the family line had reached its nadir in me. "But maybe you're a right smart occupied of a night, I don't know." He raked a large cud of tobacco out of his cheek with his forefinger and spat.

He looked around with the air of a man completing an inspection, which is exactly what he was doing. "Well, it looks like you're making a little headway. You got it looking some better. Here," he said, pawing among a litter of paper, tools, and other odds and ends on top of the dashboard and then on the seat beside him, "I brought you something." He eventually forceped forth an old newspaper page folded into a tight rectangle the size of a wallet and handed it through the truck window. "You ought to have it. It ain't no good to me. The madam, you know, is hell for an antique. She bought an old desk at a sale, and that was in one of the drawers."

I unfolded the paper and read the headline: BEN FELTNER, FRIEND TO ALL, SHOT DEAD IN PORT WILLIAM.

"Ben Feltner was your great-granddaddy."

"Yes. I know."

"I remember him. He was fine as they come. They never made 'em no finer. The last man on earth you'd a thought would get shot."

"So I've heard."

"Thad Coulter was a good kind of feller, too, far as that goes. I don't reckon he was the kind you'd a thought would shoot somebody, either."

He pushed his hat back and scratched his forehead. "One of them things," he said. "They happen."

He scratched his head some more and propped his wrist on top of the steering wheel, letting the hand dangle. "Tell you," he said, "there ain't a way in this world to know what a human creature is going to do next. I loaned a feller five hundred dollars once. He was a good feller, too, wasn't a thing wrong with him far as I knew, I liked him. And dogged if he didn't kill himself fore it was a week." "Killed himself," I said.

"*Killed* himself," Braymer said. He meditated a moment, looking off at his memory of the fellow and wiggling two of the fingers that hung over the steering wheel. "Don't you know," he said, "not wishing him no bad luck, but I wished he'd a done it a week or two sooner."

I laughed.

"Well," he said, "I know you want to be at work. I'll get out of your way."

I said, "Don't be in a hurry," but he was starting the truck and didn't hear me. I called, "Thanks!" as he backed around. He raised his hand, not looking at me, and drove away, steering with both hands, with large deliberate motions, as if the truck were the size of a towboat.

There was an upturned feed bucket just inside the barn door. I sat down on it and unfolded the paper again. It was the front page of the Hargrave *Weekly Express,* flimsy and yellow, nearly illegible in some of the creases. It told how, on a Saturday morning in the July of 1912, Ben Feltner, who so far as was known had had no enemies, had been killed by a single shot to the head from a .22 caliber revolver. His assailant, Thad Coulter, had said, upon turning himself in to the sheriff at Hargrave soon after the incident, "I've killed the best friend I ever had." It was not a long article. It told about the interment of Ben Feltner and named his survivors. It told nothing that I did not know, and I knew little more than it told. I knew that Thad Coulter had killed himself in jail, shortly after the murder. And I knew that he was my grandfather Catlett's first cousin.

I had learned that much, not from anyone's attempt, ever, to tell me the story, but from bits and pieces dropped out of conversations among my elders, in and out of the family. Once, for instance, I heard my mother say to my father that she had always been troubled by the thought of Thad Coulter's lonely anguish as he prepared to kill himself in the Hargrave jail. I had learned what I knew, the bare outline of the event, without asking questions, both fearing the pain that I knew surrounded the story and honoring the silence that surrounded the pain.

But sitting in the barn that morning, looking at the old page opened on my knees, I saw how incomplete the story was as the article told it and as I knew it. And seeing it so, I felt incomplete myself. I suddenly wanted to go and see my grandfather. I did not intend to question him. I had never heard him speak so much as a word about his father's death, and I could not have imagined breaking his silence. I only wanted to be in his presence, as if in his presence I could somehow enter into the presence of an agony that I knew had shaped us all.

With the paper folded again in my shirt pocket, I drove the two miles to Port William and turned in under the old maples beside the house. When I let myself in, the house was quiet, and I went as quietly as I could to my grandfather's room, thinking he might be asleep. But he was awake, his fingers laced together on top of the bedclothes. He had seen me drive in and was watching the door when I entered the room.

"Morning," I said.

He said, "Morning, son," and lifted one of his hands.

"How're you feeling?"

"Still feeling."

I sat down in the rocker by the bed and told him, in Braymer's words, the story of the too-late suicide.

My grandfather laughed. "I expect that grieved Braymer."

"Is Braymer pretty tight?" I asked, knowing he was.

"I wouldn't say 'tight,' but he'd know the history of every dollar he ever made. Braymer's done a lot of hard work."

My grandmother had heard us talking, and now she called me. "Oh, Andy!"

"I'll be back," I said, and went to see what she wanted.

She was sitting in the small bedroom by the kitchen where she had always done her sewing and where she slept now that my grandfather was ill. She was sitting by the window in the small cane-bottomed rocking chair that was her favorite. Her hands were lying on her lap and she was not rocking. I knew that her arthritis was hurting her; otherwise, at that time of day she would have been busy at something. She had medicine for the arthritis, but it made her feel unlike herself; up to a certain point of endurability, she preferred the pain. She sat still and let the pain go its way and occupied her mind with thoughts. Or that is what she said she did. I believed, and I was as sure as if she had told me, that when she sat alone that way, hurting or not, she was praying. Though I never heard her pray aloud in my life, it seems to me now that I can reproduce in my mind the very voice of her prayers.

She had called me in to find out things, which was her way. I sat down on the stool in front of her and submitted to examination. She wanted to know what Flora was doing, and what the children were doing, and when I had seen my mother, and what she had been doing. She asked exacting questions that called for much detail in the answers, watching me intently to see that I withheld nothing. She did not tolerate secrets, even the most considerate ones. She had learned that we sometimes omitted or rearranged facts to keep her from worrying, but her objection to that was both principled and passionate. If we were worried, she wanted to worry with us; it was her place, she said.

After a while, she quit asking questions but continued to look at me. And then she said, "You're thinking about something you're not saying. What is it? Tell Granny."

She had said that to me many times in the thirty years I had known her. By then, I thought it was funny. But if I was no longer intimidated, I was still compelled. In thirty years I had never been able to deceive her when she was looking straight at me. I could have lied, but she would have known it and then would have supposed that somebody was sick. I laughed and handed her the paper out of my pocket.

"Braymer Hardy brought that to me this morning."

She unfolded it, read a little of the article but not all, and folded it back up. Her hands lay quiet in her lap again, and she looked out the window, though obviously not seeing what was out there that morning. Another morning had come to her, and she was seeing it again through the interval of fifty-three years.

"It's a wonder," she said, "that Mat didn't kill Thad Coulter that morning."

I said, "Granddad?"

And then she told me the story. She told it quietly, looking through the window into that July morning in 1912. Her hands lay in her lap and never moved. The only effect her telling had on her was a glistening that appeared from time to time in her eyes. She told the story well, giving many details. She had a good memory, and she had lived many years with her mother-in-law, who also had a good one. I have the impression that they, but not my grandfather, had pondered together over the event many times. She spoke as if she were seeing it all happen, even the parts of it that she had in fact not seen.

"If it hadn't been for Jack Beechum, Mat *would* have killed him," my grandmother said.

That was the point. Or it was one of the points—the one, perhaps, that she most wanted me to see. But it was not the beginning of the story. Adam and Eve and then Cain and Abel began it, as my grandmother depended on me to know. Even in Thad Coulter's part of the story, the beginning was some years earlier than the July of 1912.

Abner Coulter, Thad's only son, had hired himself out to a grocer in Hargrave. After a few years, when he had (in his own estimation) learned the trade, he undertook to go into business for himself in competition with his former employer. He rented a building right on the courthouse square. He was enabled to do this by a sizable sum of money borrowed from the Hargrave bank on a note secured by a mortgage on his father's farm.

And here Thad's character enters into the story. For Thad not only secured his son's note with the farm that was all he had in the world and that he had only recently finished paying for but he further committed himself by bragging in Port William of his son's new status as a merchant in the county seat.

"Thad Coulter was not a bad man," my grandmother said. "I believed then, and I believe now, that he was not a bad man. But we are all as little children. Some know it and some don't."

She looked at me to see if I was one who knew it, and I nodded, but I was thirty then and did not know it yet.

"He was as a little child," she said, "and he was in serious trouble."

He had in effect given his life and its entire effort as hostage to the possibility that Abner, his only son, could be made a merchant in a better place than Port William.

Before two years were out, Abner repaid his father's confidence by converting many small private fritterings and derelictions into an undisguisable public failure and thereupon by riding off to somewhere unknown on the back of a bay gelding borrowed ostensibly for an overnight trip to Port William. And so Thad's fate was passed from the reckless care of his son to the small mercy of the law. Without more help than he could confidently expect, he was going to lose his farm. Even with help, he was going to have to pay for it again, and he was close to sixty years old.

As he rode home from his interview with the Hargrave banker, in which the writing on the wall had been made plain to him, he was gouging his heel urgently into his mule's flank. Since he had got up out of the chair in the banker's office, he had been full of a desire as compelling as thirst to get home, to get stopped, to get low to the ground, as if to prevent himself from falling off the world. For the country that he had known all his life and had depended on, at least in dry weather, to be solid and steady underfoot had suddenly risen under him like a wave.

Needing help as he did, he could not at first bring himself to ask for it. Instead, he spent most of two days propped against a post in his barn, drinking heavily and talking aloud to himself about betrayal, ruin, the coldheartedness of the Hargrave bankers, and the poor doings of damned fools, meaning both Abner and himself. And he recalled, with shocks of bitterness that only the whiskey could assuage, his confident words in Port William about Abner and his prospects.

"I worked for it, and I come to own it," he said over and over again. "Now them will own it that never worked for it. And him that stood on it to mount up into the world done run to perdition without a patch, damn him, to cover his ass or a rag to hide his face."

When his wife and daughter begged him to come into the house, he said that a man without the sense to keep a house did not deserve to be in one. He said he would shelter with the dogs and hogs, where he belonged.

The logical source of help was Ben Feltner. Ben had helped Thad to buy his farm—had signed his note and stood behind him. Ben was his friend, and friendship mattered to Ben; it may have mattered to him above all. But Thad did not go to Ben until after his second night in the barn. He walked to Ben's house in Port William early in the morning, drunk and unsteady, his mind tattered and raw from repeated plunges through the thorns and briars of his ruin.

Ben was astonished by the look of him. Thad had always been a man who used himself hard, and he had grown gaunt and stooped, his mouth slowly caving in as he lost his teeth. But that morning he was also soiled, sagging, unshaved and uncombed, his eyes bloodshot and glary. But Ben said, "Come in, Thad. Come in and sit down." And he took him by the arm, led him in to a chair, and sat down facing him.

"They got me, Ben," Thad said, the flesh twitching around his eyes. "They done got me to where I can't get loose." His eyes glazed by tears that never fell, he made as much sense of his calamity as he was able to make: "A poor man don't stand no show." And then, his mind lurching on, unable to stop, he fell to cursing, first Abner, and then the Hargrave bank, and then the ways of the world that afforded no show to a poor man.

Ben listened to it all, sitting with his elbow on the chair arm and his forefinger pointed against his cheek. Thad's language and his ranting in that place would not have been excusable had he been sober. But insofar Thad was drunk, Ben was patient. He listened attentively, his eyes on Thad's face, except that from time to time he looked down at his beard as if to give Thad an opportunity to see that he should stop.

Finally Ben stopped him. "Thad, I'll tell you what. I don't believe I can talk with you anymore this morning. Go home, now, and get sober and come back. And then we'll see."

Thad did not have to take Ben's words as an insult. But in his circumstances and condition, it was perhaps inevitable that he would. That Ben was his friend made the offense worse—far worse. In refusing to talk to him as he was, Ben, it seemed to Thad, had exiled him from the society of human beings, had withdrawn the last vestige of a possibility that he might find anywhere a redemption for himself, much less for his forfeited land. For Thad was not able then to distinguish between himself as he was and himself as he might be sober. He saw himself already as a proven fool, fit only for the company of dogs and hogs. If he could have accepted this judgment of himself, then his story would at least have been different and would perhaps have been better. But while he felt the force and truth of his own judgment, he raged against it. He had fled to Ben, hoping that somehow, by some means that he could not imagine, Ben could release him from the solitary cage of his self-condemnation. And now Ben had shut the door.

Thad's whole face began to twitch and his hands to move aimlessly, as if his body were being manipulated from the inside by some intention that he could not control. Patches of white appeared under his whiskers. He said, "I cuss you to your damned face, Ben Feltner, for I have come to you with my hat in my hand and you have spit in it. You have throwed in your lot with them sons of bitches against me."

At that Ben reached his limit. Yet even then he did not become angry. He was a large, unfearful man, and his self-defense had something of merriment in it. He stood up. "Now, Thad, my friend," he said, "you must go." And he helped him to the door. He did not do so violently or with an excess of force. But though he was seventy-two years old, Ben was still in hearty strength, and he helped Thad to the door in such a way that Thad had no choice but to go.

But Thad did not go home. He stayed, hovering about the front of the house, for an hour or more.

"It seemed like hours and hours that he stayed out there," my grandmother said. She and my great-grandmother, Nancy, and old Aunt Cass, the cook, had overheard the conversation between Ben and Thad, or had overheard at least Thad's part of it, and afterward they watched him from the windows, for his fury had left an influence. The house was filled with a quiet that seemed to remember with sorrow the quiet that had been in it before Thad had come.

The morning was bright and still, and it was getting hot, but Thad seemed unable to distinguish between sun and shade. There had got to be something fluttery or mothlike about him now, so erratic and unsteady and unceasing were his movements. He was talking to himself, nodding or shaking his head, his hands making sudden strange motions without apparent reference to whatever he might have been saying. Now and again he started resolutely toward the house and then swerved away.

All the while the women watched. To my grandmother, remembering, it seemed that they were surrounded by signs that had not yet revealed their significance. Aunt Cass told her afterward, "I dreamed of the dark, Miss

Margaret, all full of the sound of crying, and I knowed it was something bad." And it seemed to my grandmother, as she remembered, that she too had felt the house and town and the bright day itself all enclosed in that dreamed darkness full of the sounds of crying.

Finally, looking out to where the road from upriver came over the rise into town, they saw a team and wagon coming. Presently they recognized Thad Coulter's team, a pair of mare mules, one black and the other once gray but now faded to white. They were driven by Thad's daughter, wearing a sunbonnet, a sun-bleached blue cotton dress, and an apron.

"It's Martha Elizabeth," Nancy said.

And Aunt Cass said, "Poor child."

"Well," Nancy said, relieved, "she'll take him home."

When Martha Elizabeth came to where Thad was, she stopped the mules and got down. So far as they could see from the house, she did not plead with him. She did not say anything at all. She took hold of him, turned him toward the wagon, and led him to it. She held onto him as he climbed unsteadily up into the wagon and sat down on the spring seat, and then, gathering her skirts in one hand, she climbed up and sat beside him. And all the while she was gentle with him. Afterward and always, my grandmother remembered how gentle Martha Elizabeth had been with him.

Martha Elizabeth turned the team around, and the Feltner women watched the wagon with its troubled burden go slowly back along the ridge-line. When it had disappeared, they went back to their housework.

Ben, who had meant to go to the field where his hands were at work, did not leave the house as long as Thad was waiting about outside. He saw no point in antagonizing Thad when he did not have to, and so he sat down with a newspaper.

When he knew that Thad was gone and had had time to be out of sight, Ben got up and put on his hat and went out. He was worried about the state both of Thad's economy and of his mind. He thought he might find some of the other Coulters in town. He didn't know that he would, but it was Saturday, and he probably would.

The Feltner house stood, as it still does, in the overlap of the northeast corner of the town and the southwest corner of Ben's farm, which spread away from the house and farmstead over the ridges and hollows and down the side of the valley to the river. There was a farmstead at each of the town's four corners. There was, as there still is, only the one road, which climbed out of the river valley, crossed a mile of ridge, passed through the town, and, after staying on the ridge another half mile or so, went back down into the valley again. For most of its extent, at that time, it was little more than a wagon track. Most of the goods that reached the Port William merchants still came to the town landing by steamboat and then up the hill by team and wagon. The town itself consisted of perhaps two dozen houses, a church, a blacksmith shop, a bank, a barber shop, a doctor's office, a hotel, two saloons, and four stores that sold a variety of merchandise from groceries to dry goods to hardware to harness. The road that passed through town was there only as a casual and hardly fore-seen result of the comings and goings of the inhabitants. An extemporaneous town government had from time to time caused a few loads of creek rock to be hauled and knapped and spread over it, and the townspeople had flung their ashes into it, but that was all. It had never thought of calling itself a street.

Though the houses and shops had been connected for some time by tele-phone lines carried overhead on peeled and whitewashed locust poles, there was as yet not an automobile in the town. There were times in any year still when Port William could not have been reached by an automobile that was not accompanied by a team of mules to pull it across the creeks and out of the mud holes.

Except for the telephone lines, the town, as it looked to Ben Feltner on that July morning seventy-eight years ago, might have been unchanged for many more years than it had existed. It looked older than its history. And yet in Port William, as everywhere else, it was already the second decade of the twentieth century. And in some of the people of the town and the community surrounding it, one of the characteristic diseases of the twentieth century was making its way: the suspicion that they would be greatly improved if they were someplace else. This disease had entered into Thad Coulter and into Abner. In Thad it was fast coming to crisis. If Port William could not save him, then surely there was another place that could. But Thad could not just leave, as Abner had; Port William had been too much his life for that. And he was held also by friendship—by his friendship for Ben Feltner, and for him-self as a man whom Ben Feltner had befriended—a friendship that Ben Felt-ner seemed now to have repudiated and made hateful. Port William was a stumbling block to Thad, and he must rid himself of it somehow.

Ben, innocent of the disease that afflicted his friend yet mortally impli-cated in it and not knowing it, made his way down into the town, looking about in order to gauge its mood—for Port William had its moods, and they needed watching. More energy was generated in the community than the work of the community could consume, and the surplus energy often went into fighting. There had been cuttings and shootings enough. But usually the fighting was more primitive, and the combatants simply threw whatever pro-jectiles came to hand: corncobs, snowballs, green walnuts, or rocks. In the previous winter, a young Coulter by the name of Burley had claimed that he had had an eye blackened by a frozen horse turd thrown, so far as he could determine, by a Power of the Air. But the place that morning was quiet. Most of the crops had been laid by and many of the farmers were already in town, feeling at ease and inclined to rest now that their annual battle with the weeds had ended. They were sitting on benches and kegs or squatting on their heels under the shade trees in front of the stores, or standing in pairs or small groups among the hitched horses along the sides of the road. Ben passed among them, greeting them and pausing to talk, enjoying himself, and all the while on the lookout for one or another of the Coulters.

Martha Elizabeth was Thad's youngest, the last at home. She had, he thought, the levelest head of any of his children and was the best. Assuming the authority that his partiality granted her, she had at fifteen taken charge of the household, supplanting her mother, who was sickly, and her three older sisters, who had married and gone. At seventeen, she was responsible beyond her years. She was a tall, raw-boned girl, with large hands and feet, a red complexion, and hair so red that, in the sun, it appeared to be on fire.

"Everybody loved Martha Elizabeth," my grandmother said. "She was as good as ever was."

To Thad it was a relief to obey her, to climb into the wagon under the pressure of her hand on his arm and to sit beside her as she drove the team homeward through the rising heat of the morning. Her concern for him gave him shelter. Holding to the back of the seat, he kept himself upright and, for the moment, rested in being with her.

But when they turned off the ridge onto the narrower road that led down into the valley called Cattle Pen and came in sight of their place, she could no longer shelter him. It had long been, to Thad's eye, a pretty farm—a hundred or so acres of slope and ridge on the west side of the little valley, the lower, gentler slopes divided from the ridge land by a ledgy bluff that was wooded, the log house and other buildings occupying a shelf above the creek bottom. Through all his years of paying for it, he had aspired toward it as toward a Promised Land. To have it, he had worked hard and long and deprived himself, and Rachel, his wife, had deprived herself. He had worked alone more often than not. Abner, as he grew able, had helped, as the girls had, also. But Abner had been reserved for something better. Abner was smart—too smart, as Thad and Rachel agreed, without ever much talking about it, to spend his life farming a hillside. Something would have to be done to start him on his way to something better, a Promised Land yet more distant.

Although he had thought the farm not good enough for Abner, Thad was divided in his mind; for himself he loved it. It was what he had transformed his life into. And now, even in the morning light, it lay under the shadow of his failure, and he could not bear to look at it. It was his life, and he was no longer in it. Somebody else, some other thing that did not even know it, stood to take possession of it. He was ashamed in its presence. To look directly at it would be like looking Martha Elizabeth full in the eyes, which he could not do either. And his shame raged in him.

When she stopped in the lot in front of the barn and helped him down, he started unhitching the team. But she took hold of his arm and drew him away gently toward the house.

"Come on, now," she said. "You've got to have you something to eat and some rest."

But he jerked away from her. "Go see to your mammy!"

"No," she said. "Come on." And she attempted again to move him toward the house.

He pushed her away, and she fell. He could have cut off his hand for so misusing her, and yet his rage at himself included her. He reached into the wagon box and took out a short hickory stock with a braid of rawhide knotted to it. He shook it at her.

"Get up," he said. "Get yonder to that house 'fore I wear you out."

He had never spoken to her in such a way, had never imagined himself doing so. He hated what he had done, and he could not undo it.

The heat of the day had established itself now. There was not a breeze anywhere, not a breath. A still haze filled the valley and redoubled the light. Within that blinding glare he occupied a darkness that was loud with accusing cries.

Martha Elizabeth stood at the kitchen door a moment, looking back at him, and then she went inside. Thad turned back to the team then, unhitched them, did up the lines, and led the mules to their stalls in the barn. He moved as if dreaming through these familiar motions that had now estranged themselves from him. The closer he had come to home, the more the force of his failure had gathered there to exclude him.

And it was Ben Feltner who had barred the door and left him without a friend. Ben Feltner, who owed nothing, had turned his back on his friend, who now owed everything.

He said aloud, "Yes, I'll come back sober, God damn you to Hell!"

He lifted the jug out of the white mule's manger, pulled the cob from its mouth, and drank. When he lowered it, it was empty. It had lasted him three days, and now it was empty. He cocked his wrist and broke the jug against an upright.

"Well, that does for you, old holler-head."

He stood, letting the whiskey seek its level in him, and felt himself slowly come into purpose; now he had his anger full and clear. Now he was summoned by an almost visible joy.

He went to the house, drank from the water bucket on the back porch, and stepped through the kitchen door. Rachel and Martha Elizabeth were standing together by the cookstove, facing him.

"Thad, honey, I done fixed dinner," Rachel said. "Set down and eat."

He opened the stairway door, stepped up, and took down his pistol from the little shelf over the door frame.

"No, now," Martha Elizabeth said. "Put that away. You ain't got a use in this world for that."

"Don't contrary me," Thad said. "Don't you say another damned word."

He put the pistol in his hip pocket with the barrel sticking up and turned to the door.

"Wait, Thad," Rachel said. "Eat a little before you go." But she was already so far behind him that he hardly heard her.

He walked to the barn, steadying himself by every upright thing he came to, so that he proceeded by a series of handholds on doorjamb and porch post and gatepost and tree. He could no longer see the place but walked in a shifting aisle of blinding light through a cloud of darkness. Behind him now was almost nothing. And ahead of him was the singular joy to which his heart now beat in answer.

He went into the white mule's stall, unbuckled hame strap and bellyband, and shoved the harness off her back, letting it fall. He unbuckled the collar and let it fall. Again his rage swelled within him, seeming to tighten the skin of his throat, as though his body might fail to contain it, for he had never before in his life allowed a mule's harness to touch the ground if he could help it. But he was not in his life now, and his rage pleased him.

He hooked his finger in the bit ring and led the mule to the drinking trough by the well in front of the barn. The trough was half an oak barrel, nearly full of water. The mule wanted to drink, but he jerked her head up and drew her forward until she stood beside the trough. The shorn stubble of her mane under his hand, he stepped up onto the rim. Springing, he cast himself across the mule's back, straddled her, and sat upright as darkness swung around him. He jerked hard at the left rein.

"Get up, Beck," he said.

The mule was as principled as a martyr. She would have died before she would have trotted a step, and yet he urged her forward with his heel. Even as the hind feet of the mule lifted from their tracks, the thought of Martha Elizabeth formed itself within the world's ruin. She seemed to rise up out of its shambles, like a ghost or an influence. She would follow him. He needed to hurry.

On the fringe of the Saturday bustle in front of the business houses, Ben met Early Rowanberry and his little boy, Arthur. Early was carrying a big sack, and Art a small one. They had started out not long after breakfast; from the log house on the ridgetop where the Rowanberrys had settled before Kentucky was a state, they had gone down the hill, forded the creek known as Sand Ripple, and then walked up the Shade Branch hollow through the Feltner Place and on to town. Early had done his buying and a little talking, had bought a penny's worth of candy for Art, and now they were starting the long walk back. Ben knew that they had made the trip on foot to spare their mules, though the sacks would weigh sorely on their shoulders before they made it home.

"Well, Early," Ben said, "you've got a good hand with you today, I see."

"He's tol'ble good company, Ben, and he packs a little load," Early said.

Ben liked all the Rowanberrys, who had been good neighbors to him all his life, and Early was a better-than-average Rowanberry—a quiet man with a steady gaze and a sort of local fame for his endurance at hard work.

Ben then offered his hand to Art, who shyly held out his own. But then Ben said, "My boy, are you going to grow up to be a wheelhorse like your pap?" and Art answered without hesitation, "Yes, sir."

"Ah, that's right," Ben said. And he placed his hand on the boy's unladen shoulder.

The two Rowanberrys then resumed their homeward journey, and Ben walked on down the edge of the dusty road into town.

Ben was in no hurry. He had his mission in mind and was somewhat anxious about it, but he gave it its due place in the order of things. Thad's difficulty was not simple; whatever it was possible to do for him could not be done in a hurry. Ben passed slowly through the talk of the place and time, partaking of it. He liked the way the neighborhood gathered into itself on such days. Now and then, in the midst of the more casual conversation, a little trade talk would rouse up over a milk cow or a pocketknife or a saddle or a horse or mule. Or there would be a joke or a story or a bit of news, uprisings of the town's interest in itself that would pass through it and die away like scurries of wind. It was close to noon. It was hot even in the shade now, and the smells of horse sweat and horse manure had grown strong. On the benches and kegs along the storefronts, pocketknives were busy. Profound meditations were coming to bear upon long scrolls of cedar or poplar curling backward over thumbs and wrists and piling over shoetops.

Somebody said, "Well, I can see the heat waves a-rising."

Somebody else said, "Ain't nobody but a lazy man can see them heat waves."

And then Ben saw Thad's cousin, Dave Coulter, and Dave's son, Burley, coming out of one of the stores, Dave with a sack of flour on his shoulder and Burley with a sack of meal on his. Except for his boy's face and grin, Burley was a grown man. He was seventeen, a square-handed, muscular fellow already known for the funny things he said, though his elders knew of them only by hearsay. He and his father turned down the street toward their wagon, and Ben followed them.

When they had hunched the sacks off their shoulders into the wagon, Ben said, "Dave?"

Dave turned to him and stuck out his hand. "Why, howdy, Ben."

"How are you, Dave?"

"'Bout all right, I reckon."

"And how are you, Burley?"

Dave turned to his boy to see that he would answer properly; Burley, grinning, said, "Doing about all right, thank you, sir," and Dave turned back to Ben.

"Had to lay in a little belly timber," he said, "'gainst we run plumb out. And the boy here, he wanted to come see the sights."

"Well, my boy," Ben said, "have you learned anything worthwhile?"

Burley grinned again, gave a quick nod, and said, "Yessir."

"Oh, hit's an educational place," Dave said. "We hung into one of them educational conversations yonder in the store. That's why we ain't hardly going to make it back home by dinnertime."

"Well, I won't hold you up for long," Ben said. And he told Dave as much as he had understood of Thad's trouble. They were leaning against the wagon box, facing away from the road. Burley, who had gone to untie the mules, was still standing at their heads.

"Well," Dave said, "hit's been norated around that Abner weren't doing just the way he ought to. Tell you the truth, I been juberous about that loan proposition ever since Thad put his name to it. Put his whole damned foothold in that damned boy's pocket is what he done. And now you say it's all gone up the spout."

"He's in a serious fix, no question about it."

"Well, is there anything a feller can do for him?"

"Well, there's one thing for certain. He was drunk when he came to see me. He was cussing and raring. If you, or some of you, could get him sober, it would help. And then we could see if we can help him out of his scrape."

"Talking rough, was he?"

"Rough enough."

"I'm sorry, Ben. Thad don't often drink, but when he does he drinks like the Lord appointed him to get rid of it all."

Somebody said, "Look out!"

They turned to see Thad and the white mule almost abreast of them. Thad was holding the pistol.

"They said he just looked awful," my grandmother said. "He looked like death warmed over."

Ben said, without raising his voice, in the same reasonable tone in which he had been speaking to Dave, "Hold on, Thad."

And Thad fired.

Dave saw a small round red spot appear in the center of Ben's forehead. A perplexed look came to his face, as if he had been intending to say something more and had forgot what it was. For a moment, he remained standing just as he had been, one hand on the rim of the wagon box. And then he fell. As he went down, his shoulder struck the hub of the wagon wheel so that he fell onto his side, his hat rolling underneath the wagon.

Thad put the pistol back into his pocket. The mule had stood as still after he had halted her as if she were not there at all but at home under a tree in the pasture. When Thad kicked her, she went on again.

Ben Feltner never had believed in working on Sunday, and he did not believe in not working on workdays. Those two principles had shaped all his weeks. He liked to make his hay cuttings and begin other large, urgent jobs as early in the week as possible in order to have them finished before Sunday. On Saturdays, he and Mat and the hands worked in the crops if necessary; otherwise, that day was given to the small jobs of maintenance that the farm constantly required and to preparations for Sunday, when they would do nothing except milk and feed. When the work was caught up and the farm in order, Ben liked to have everybody quit early on Saturday afternoon. He liked the quiet that descended over the place then, with the day of rest ahead.

On that Saturday morning he had sent Old Smoke, Aunt Cass's husband, and their son, Samp, and Samp's boy, Joe, to mend a fence back on the river bluff. Mat he sent to the blacksmith shop to have the shoes reset on Governor, his buggy horse. They would not need Governor to go to church; they walked to church. But when they had no company on Sunday afternoon and the day was fair, Ben and Nancy liked to drive around the neighborhood, looking at the crops and stopping at various households to visit. They liked especially to visit Nancy's brother, Jack Beechum, and his wife, Ruth, who lived on the Beechum home place, the place that Nancy would always refer to as "out home."

And so Mat that morning, after his chores were done, had slipped a halter on Governor and led him down through town to the blacksmith's. He had to wait—there were several horses and mules already in line—and so he tied Governor to the hitch rail in front of the shop and went in among the others who were waiting and talking, figuring that he would be late for dinner.

It was a good place. The shop stood well back from the street, leaving in front of it a tree-shaded, cinder-covered yard, which made room for the hitch rail and for the wagons, sleds, and other implements waiting to be repaired. The shop itself was a single large, dirt-floored room, meticulously clean—every surface swept and every tool in place. Workbenches went around three walls. Near the large open doorway were the forge and anvil.

The blacksmith—a low, broad, grizzled man by the name of Elder Johnson—was the best within many miles, a fact well known to himself, which sometimes made him difficult. He also remembered precisely every horse or mule he had ever nailed a shoe on, and so he was one of the keepers of the town's memory.

Elder was shoeing a colt that was nervous and was giving him trouble. He was working fast so as to cause the colt as little discomfort as he could. He picked up the left hind hoof, caught it between his aproned knees, and laid the shoe on it. The shoe was too wide at the heel, and he let the colt's foot go back to the floor. A small sharp-faced man smoking a cob pipe was waiting, holding out a broken singletree for Elder's inspection as he passed on his way back to the forge.

Elder looked as if the broken tree were not the sort of thing that could concern him.

"Could I get this done by this evening?" the man asked. His name was Skeets Willard, and his work was always in some state of emergency. "I can't turn a wheel," he said, "til I get that fixed."

Elder let fall the merest glance at the two pieces of the singletree, and then looked point-blank at the man himself as if surprised not only by his presence but by his existence. "What the hell do you think I am? A hammer with a brain? Do you see all them horses and mules tied up out there? If you want that fixed, I'll fix it when I can. If you don't, take it home."

Skeets Willard elected to lay the pieces down in a conspicuous place by the forge. And Elder, whose outburst had not interrupted the flow of talk among the bystanders, caught the shoe in his tongs and shoved it in among the coals of the forge. He cranked the bellows and made small flames spike up out of the coals. As he turned the handle, he stared in a kind of trance at the light of the open doorway, and the light shone in his eyes, and his face and his arms were shining with sweat. Presently he drew the shoe, glowing, out of the coals and, laying it on the horn of the anvil, turned in the heel. He then plunged the shoe into the slack tub from which it raised a brief shriek of steam.

Somebody turned out of the conversation and said, "Say, Elder, do you remember that little red mule come in here with a bunch of yearlings Marce Catlett bought up around Lexington? Ned, I think they called him."

"Newt," Elder said in so even a voice that Skeets Willard might never have been there. "You bet I remember him."

He took the cooled shoe from the slack tub and, picking up the colt's foot and straddling it again, quickly nailed one nail in each side, raking the points over with the claws of his hammer. He let the colt stand on his foot again to see how the shoe set. "You bet I remember him," he said. "That mule could kick the lard out of a biscuit."

And then they heard the single voice raised in warning out in the road, followed immediately by the shot and by a rising murmur of excited indistinguishable voices as the whole Saturday crowd turned its attention to the one thing.

Mat hurried out with the others and saw the crowd wedged in between the storefronts and Dave Coulter's wagon. He only began to realize that the occasion concerned him when the crowd began to make way for him as he approached.

"Let him through! Let him through!" the crowd said.

The crowd opened to let him through, turning its faces to him, falling silent as it saw who he was. And then he saw what was left of the man who had been his father lying against the wagon wheel. Those nearest him heard him say, "Oh!" and it did not sound like him at all. He stepped forward and knelt and took his father's wrist in his hand to feel for the pulse that he did not expect, having seen the wound and the fixed unsighted eyes. The crowd now was as quiet around him as the still treetops along the road. For what seemed a long time Mat knelt there with his father's dead wrist in his hand, while his mind arrived and arrived and yet arrived at that place and time and that body lying still on the soiled and bloodied stones. When he looked up again, he did not look like the man they had known at all.

"Who did this?" he said

And the crowd answered, "Thad Coulter, he done it."

"Where'd he go?"

"He taken down the road yonder towards Hargrave. He was on that old white mule, old May."

When Mat stood up again from his father's side, he was a man new-created by rage. All that he had been and thought and done gave way to his one desire to kill the man who had killed his father.

He ached, mind and body, with the elation of that one thought. He was not armed, but he never thought of that. He would go for the horse he had left tied at the blacksmith's. He would ride Thad Coulter down. He would come up beside him and club him off the mule. He would beat him down out of the air. And in that thought, which lived more in his right arm than in his head, both he and his enemy were as clear of history as if newborn.

By the time Mat was free of the crowd, he was running.

Jack Beechum had sold a team of mules the day before, and so he had a check to carry to the bank. He also had a list of things that Ruth wanted from town, and now that he had money ahead he wanted to settle his account at Chatham's store. His plan was to do his errands in town and get back home by dinner; that afternoon, he wanted to mow a field of hay, hoping it would cure by Monday. He rode to town on a good black gelding, called Socks for his four white pasterns.

He tied the horse some distance from the center of town in a place of better shade and fewer flies. He went to the bank first and then went about gathering the things that Ruth needed, ending up at Chatham's. He was sitting by Beater Chatham's desk in the back, watching Beater total up his account, when they heard the shot out in the street.

"Sounds like they're getting Saturday started out there," Jack said.

"I reckon," Beater said, checking his figures.

"They're going to keep on until they shoot somebody who don't deserve it."

Beater looked at him then over the tops of his glasses. "Well, they'll have to look around outside town to find somebody, wont they?" He filled out a check for the amount of the bill and handed the check to Jack for him to sign.

And then someone who had just stepped out of the store stepped back in again and said, "Jack, you'd better come. They've shot Ben Feltner."

Jack never signed the check that day or for several days. He ran to the door. When he was outside, he saw first the crowd and then Mat running toward him out of it. Without breaking his own stride, he caught Mat and held him.

They were both moving at the same speed, and the crowd heard the shock of the impact as the two men came together. Jack could hardly have known what he was doing. He had had no time to think. He may have been moved by an impulse simply to stop things until he *could* think. Or perhaps he knew by the look on Mat's face that he had to be obstructed. At any rate, as soon as Jack had taken hold of Mat, he understood that he *had* to hold him. And he knew that he had never taken hold of any such thing before. He had caught Mat in a sideways hug that clamped his arms to his sides. Jack's sole task was to keep Mat from freeing his arms. But Mat was little more than half Jack's age; he was in the prime of his strength. And now he twisted and strained with the concentration of fury, uttering cries that could have been either grunts or sobs, forcing Jack both to hold him and to hold him up. They strove there a long time, heaving and staggering, hardly moving from the tracks they had stood in when they came together, and the dust rose up around them. Jack felt that his arms would pull apart at the joints. He ached afterward. Something went out of him that day, and he was not the same again.

And what went out of Jack came into Mat. Or so it seemed, for in that desperate embrace he became a stronger man than he had been. A strength came into him that held his grief and his anger as Jack had held him. And Jack knew of the coming of this strength, not because it enabled Mat to break free but because it enabled Jack to turn him loose. Mat ceased to strive, and Jack let go his hold. He stepped away, allowing himself to be recognized, and Mat stood. To Jack, it was as though he had caught one man and let another go.

But he put his eye on Mat, not willing yet to trust him entirely to himself, and waited.

They both were winded, wet with sweat, and for a moment they only breathed, watched by the crowd, Jack watching Mat, Mat looking at nothing.

As they stood so, the girl, Martha Elizabeth, walked by in the road. She did not look at them or at the wagon or at the body crumpled on the ground. She walked past it all, looking ahead, as if she already saw what she was walking toward.

Coming aware that Jack was waiting on him, Mat looked up; he met Jack's gaze. He said, "Pa's dead. Thad Coulter has shot him."

They waited, looking at each other still, while the earth shook under them.

Mat said, "I'll go tell Ma. You bring Pa, but give me a little time."

Dinner was ready, and the men were late.

"It wasn't usual for them to be late," my grandmother said, "but we didn't think yet that anything was wrong. Your mother was just a little girl then, and she was telling us a story about a doll and a dog and a horse."

Aunt Cass stood by the stove, keeping an eye on the griddle. Nancy was sweeping the floor under the firebox of the stove; she was a woman who was always doing. Margaret, having set the table, had turned one of the chairs out into the floor and sat down. All three were listening to Bess, who presently stopped her story, rolled her eyes, and said, "I hear my innards a-growling. I reckon I must be hungry."

They laughed.

"I spect so, I spect so," Aunt Cass said. "Well, you'll get something to eat fore long."

When she heard Mat at the kitchen door, Aunt Cass said, "Miss Nancy, you want to take the hoecake up?" And then seeing the change in Mat's face, which was new to it but old to the world, she hushed and stood still. Nancy, seeing the expression on Cass's face, turned to look at Mat.

Bess said, "Goody! Now we can eat!"

Mat looked at his mother and then down at Bess and smiled. "You can eat directly," he said.

And then he said, "Margaret, take Bess and go upstairs. I think she's got a book up there she wants you to read to her."

"I knew what it was then," my grandmother said. "Oh, I felt it go all over me before I knew it in my mind. I just wanted to crawl away. But I had your mother to think about. You always have somebody to think about, and it's a blessing."

She said, "Come on, Bess, let's go read a story. We'll eat in a little bit."

As soon as he heard their footsteps going up the stairs, Mat looked at his mother again. As the silence gathered against him, he said, "Ma, I'm sorry, Pa's dead. Thad Coulter has shot him."

She was already wearing black. She had borne four children and raised one. Two of her children she had buried in the same week of a diphtheria epidemic, of which she had nearly died herself. After the third child had died, she never wore colors again. It was not that she chose to be ostentatiously bereaved. She could not have chosen to be ostentatious about anything. She was, in fact, a woman possessed of a strong native cheerfulness. And yet she had accepted a certain darkness that she had lived in too intimately to deny.

She stood, looking at Mat, while she steadied herself and steadied the room around her, in the quiet that, having suddenly begun there, would not end for a long time. And then she said to Mat, "Sit down."

She said, "Cass, sit down."

They turned chairs away from the table and sat down, and then she did.

"Now," she said, "I want to know what happened."

In the quiet Mat told as much, as little, as he knew.

As if to exert herself against the silence that too quickly filled the room, Nancy stood again. She laid her hand on the shoulder of Mat's wet shirt and patted it once.

"Cass," she said, "we mustn't cry," though there were tears on her own face.

"Mat," she said, "go get Smoke and Samp and Joe. Tell them, and tell them to come here."

To Aunt Cass again, she said, "We must fix the bed. They'll need a place to lay him."

And then they heard the burdened footsteps at the door.

In his cresting anger in the minutes before he stopped the mule in the road in Port William and fired the one shot that he ever fired in anger in his life, Thad Coulter knew a fierce, fulfilling joy. He saw the shot home to the mark, saw Ben Feltner stand a moment and go down, and then he heeled the mule hard in the side and rode on. He went on because all behind him that he might once have turned back to was gone from his mind, and perhaps even in his joy he knew that from that time there was to be no going back.

Even before the town was out of sight behind him, his anger and his joy began to leave him. It was as if his life's blood were running out of him, and he tried to stanch the flow by muttering aloud curses of his rage. But they had no force, and his depletion continued.

His first thought beyond his anger was of the mule. She was thirsty, he knew, and he had denied her a drink.

"When we get to the creek," he said.

The mule followed the windings of the road down off the upland. Below the cleared ridges, they passed through woods. On the gentler open slopes below, they came into the blank sunlight again, and he could see the river winding between its wooded banks toward its meeting with the Ohio at Hargrave.

At the foot of the hill, the road dipped under trees again and forded a creek. Thad rode the mule into the pool above the ford, loosened the rein, and let her drink. It was a quiet, deeply shaded place, the water unrippled until the mule stepped into it. For the first time in three days Thad could hear the quiet, and a bottomless sorrow opened in him, causing him suddenly to clutch his belly and groan aloud.

When the mule had finished drinking, he rode her out of the pool, dismounted, and, unbuckling one end of the rein from the bit, led her into a clump of bushes and tall weeds and tied her there. For now the thought of pursuit had come to him, and he knew he would have to go the rest of the way on foot. The mule could not be hurried, and she would be difficult to hide.

He went back to the pool and knelt at the edge of it and drank, and then he washed his hands and in his cupped hands lifted the clear water time and again to his face.

Presently, he became still, listening. He could hear nothing but the cicadas in the surrounding trees. And then he heard, coming fast, the sound of loud talking and the rapid hooftread of horses. He stepped into a patch of weeds and watched several riders go by on the road. They were boys and young men from the town who, having waited through the aftermath of the shooting, had now been carried by their excitement into pursuit of him. "Boys," he thought. He felt in no danger from them—he did not think of the pistol—and yet he feared them. He himself hurrying on foot along the road, while the young riders picked and pecked at him.

The quiet returned, and he could feel, as if in the hair roots and pores of his skin, that Martha Elizabeth was coming near. He went back to the road again.

The walking and the water drying on his face cleared his mind, and now he knew himself as he had been and as he was and knew that he was changed beyond unchanging into something he did not love. Now that his anger had drained away, his body seemed to him not only to be a burden almost too heavy to carry but to be on the verge of caving in. He walked with one hand pressed to his belly where the collapse seemed already to have begun.

The best way between Port William and Hargrave was still the river. The road found its way as if by guess, bent this way and that by the whims of typography and the convenience of landowners. At intervals, it was interrupted by farm gates.

After a while, hearing several more horses coming behind him, he stepped out of the road and lay down in a small canebrake. When they had passed, he returned to the road and went on. Always he was watchful of the houses he passed, but he stayed in the road. If he was to protect the one choice of which he was still master, he had to hurry.

And now, as he had not been able to do when he left it, he could see his farm. It shone in his mind as if inwardly lighted in the darkness that now surrounded both him and it. He could see it with the morning sun dew-bright on the woods and the sloping pastures, on the little croplands on the ridge and in the bottoms along the creek. He could see its cool shadows stretching out in the evening and the milk cows coming down the path to the barn. It was irrevocably behind him now, as if a great sword had fallen between him and it.

He was slow and small on the long road. The sun was slow overhead. The air was heavy and unmoving. He watched the steady stepping of his feet, the road going backward beneath them. He had to get out of the road only twice again: once for family in a spring wagon coming up from Hargrave and once for another horse and rider coming down from Port William. Except for those, nothing moved in the still heat but himself. Except for the cicadas, the only sounds he heard were his own steady footfalls on the dry dust.

He seemed to see always not only the changing road beneath his feet but also that other world in which he had lived, now lighted in the dark behind him, and it came to him that on that day two lives had ended for a possibility that never had existed: for Abner Coulter's mounting up in a better place. And he felt the emptiness open wider in him and again heard himself groan. He wondered, so great was the pain of that emptiness, that he did not weep, but it exceeded weeping as it exceeded words. Beyond the scope of one man's grief, it cried out in the air around him, as if in that day's hot light the trees and the fields and the dust of the road all grieved. An inward pressure that had given his body its shape seemed to have been withdrawn, and he walked, holding himself, resisting step by step the urge to bend around the emptiness opening in his middle and let himself fall.

Where the valley began to widen toward the river's mouth, the road passed a large bottom planted in corn. Thad looked back, expecting that he would see Martha Elizabeth, and he did see her. She was maybe three-quarters of a mile behind him, small in the distance, and the heat rising off the field shimmered and shook between them, but he knew her. He walked faster, and he did not look back again. It seemed to him that she knew everything he knew, and loved him anyhow. She loved him, minute by minute, not only as he had been but as he had become. It was a wonderful and a fearful thing to him that he had caused such a love for himself to come into the world and then had failed it. He could not have bowed low enough before it and remained above ground. He could not bear to think of it. But he knew that she walked behind him—balanced across the distance, in the same hot light, the same darkness, the same crying air—ever at the same speed that he walked.

Finally he came to the cluster of houses at Ellville, at the end of the bridge, and went across into Hargrave. From the bridge to the courthouse, he went ever deeper into the Saturday crowd, but he did not alter his gait or look at anybody. If anybody looked at him, he did not know it. At the cross streets, he could see on the river a towboat pushing a line of barges slowly upstream, black smoke gushing from its stacks. The walks were full of people, and the streets were full of buggies and wagons. He crossed the courthouse yard where people sat on benches or stood talking in little groups under the shade trees. It seemed to him that he walked in a world from which he had departed.

When he went through the front door of the courthouse into the sudden cool darkness of the hallway, he could not see. Lights swam in his eyes in the dark, and he had to prop himself against the wall. The place smelled of old paper and tobacco and of human beings, washed and unwashed. When he could see again, he walked to a door under a sign that said "Sheriff" and went in. It was a tall room lighted by two tall windows. There was a row of chairs for people to wait in, and several spittoons, placed at the presumed convenience of spitters, that had been as much missed as hit. No one was there but a large man in a broad-brimmed straw hat and a suit somewhat too small, who was standing behind a high desk, writing something. At first he did not look up. When he finally did look up, he stared at Thad for some time, as if not sufficiently convinced of what he saw.

"In a minute," he said and looked down again and finished what he was writing. There was a badge pinned lopsidedly to the pocket of his shirt, and he held an unlit cigar like another pen in his left hand. He said as he wrote, "You been drove hard and put up wet, I reckon."

"Yes," Thad said. "I have killed a man."

The sheriff laid the pen on the blotter and looked up. "Who?"

Thad said, "Ben Feltner, the best friend I ever had." His eyes suddenly brimmed with tears, but they did not fall. He made no sound and he did not move.

"You're a Coulter, ain't you? From up about Port William?"

"Thad," Thad said.

The sheriff would have preferred that Thad had remained a fugitive. He did not want a self-confessed murderer on his hands—especially not one fresh from a Saturday killing in Port William. He knew Ben Feltner, knew he was liked, and feared there would be a commotion. Port William, as far as he was concerned, was nothing but trouble, almost beyond the law's reach and certainly beyond its convenience—a source, as far as he was concerned, of never foreseeable bad news. He did not know what would come next, but he thought that something would, and he did not approve of it.

"I wish to hell," he said, "that everybody up there who is going to kill each other would just by God go ahead and do it." He looked at Thad for some time in silence, as if giving him an opportunity to disappear.

"Well," he said finally, "I reckon you just as well give me the pistol."

He gestured toward Thad's sagging hip pocket, and Thad took out the pistol and gave it to him.

"Come on," the sheriff said.

Thad followed him out a rear door into the small paved yard of the jail, where the sheriff rang for the jailer.

The sheriff had hardly got back into the office and taken up his work again when a motion in the doorway alerted him. He looked up and saw a big red-faced girl standing just outside the door as if uncertain whether or not it was lawful to enter. She wore a sunbonnet, a faded blue dress that reached to her ankles, and an apron. Though she was obviously timid and unused to public places, she returned his look with perfect candor.

"Come in," he said.

She crossed the threshold and again stopped.

"What can I do for you, miss?"

"I'm a-looking for Mr. Thad Coulter from up to Port William, please, sir."

"You his daughter?"

"Yes, sir."

"Well, he's here. I got him locked up. He claims he killed a fellow."

"He did," the girl said. "Is it allowed to see him?"

"Not now," the sheriff said. "You come back in the morning, miss. You can see him then."

She stood looking at him another moment, as if to make sure that he had said what he meant, and then she said, "Well, I thank you," and went out.

An hour or so later, when he shut the office and started home to supper, she was sitting on the end of one of the benches under the shade trees, looking down at her hands in her lap.

"You see," my grandmother said, "there are two deaths in this—Mr. Feltner's and Thad Coulter's. We know Mr. Feltner's because we had to know it. It was ours. That we know Thad's is because of Martha Elizabeth. The Martha Elizabeth you know."

I knew her, but it came strange to me now to think of her—to be asked to see her—as a girl. She was what I considered an old woman when I first remember her; she was perhaps eight or ten years younger than my grandmother, the fire red long gone from her hair. She was a woman always near to smiling, sometimes to laughter. Her face, it seemed, had been made to smile. It was a face that assented wholly to the being of whatever and whomever she looked at. She had gone with her father to the world's edge and had come back with this smile on her face. Miss Martha Elizabeth, we younger ones called her. Everybody loved her.

When the sheriff came back from supper, she was still there on the bench, the Saturday night shoppers and talkers, standers and passers leaving a kind of island around her, as if unwilling to acknowledge the absolute submission they sensed in her. The sheriff knew as soon as he laid eyes on her this time that she was not going to go away. Perhaps he understood that she had no place to go that she could get to before it would be time to come back.

"Come on with me," he said, and he did not sound like a sheriff now but only a man.

She got up and followed him through the hallway of the courthouse, past the locked doors of the offices, out again, and across the little iron-fenced courtyard in front of the jail. The sheriff unlocked a heavy sheet-iron door, opened it, and closed it behind them, and they were in a large room of stone, steel, and concrete, containing several cages, barred from floor to ceiling, the whole interior lighted by one kerosene lamp hanging in the corridor.

Among the bars gleaming dimly and the shadows of bars thrown back against concrete and stone, she saw her father sitting on the edge of a bunk that was only an iron shelf let down on chains from the wall, with a thin mattress laid on it. He had paid no attention when they entered. He sat still, staring at the wall, one hand pressed against his belly, the other holding to one of the chains that supported the bunk.

The sheriff opened the cell door and stood aside to let her in. "I'll come back after while," he said.

The door closed and was locked behind her, and she stood still until Thad felt her presence and looked up. When he recognized her, he covered his face with both hands.

"He put his hands over his face like a man ashamed," my grandmother said. "But he was like a man, too, who had seen what he couldn't bear."

She sat without speaking a moment, looking at me, for she had much to ask of me.

"Maybe Thad saw his guilt full and clear then. But what he saw that he couldn't bear was something else."

And again she paused, looking at me. We sat facing each other on either side of the window; my grandfather lay in one of his lengthening sleeps nearby. The old house in that moment seemed filled with a quiet that extended not only out into the whole broad morning but endlessly both ways in time.

"People sometimes talk of God's love as if it's a pleasant thing. But it is terrible, in a way. Think of all it includes. It included Thad Coulter, drunk and mean and foolish, before he killed Mr. Feltner, and it included him afterwards."

She reached out then and touched the back of my right hand with her fingers; my hand still bears that touch, invisible and yet indelible as a tattoo.

"That's what Thad saw. He saw his guilt. He had killed his friend. He had done what he couldn't undo; he had destroyed what he couldn't make. But in the same moment he saw his guilt included in love that stood as near him as Martha Elizabeth and at that moment wore her flesh. It was surely weak and wrong of him to kill himself—to sit in judgment that way over himself. But surely God's love includes people who can't bear it."

The sheriff took Martha Elizabeth home with him that night; his wife fed her and turned back the bed for her in the spare room. The next day she sat with her father in his cell.

"All that day," my grandmother said, "he would hardly take his hands from his face. Martha Elizabeth fed him what little he would eat and raised the cup to his lips for what little he would drink. And he ate and drank only because she asked him to, almost not at all. I don't know what they said. Maybe nothing."

At bedtime again that night Martha Elizabeth went home with the sheriff. When they returned to the courthouse on Monday morning, Thad Coulter was dead by his own hand.

"It's a hard story to have to know," my grandmother said. "The mercy of it was Martha Elizabeth."

She still had more to tell, but she paused again, and again she looked at me and touched my hand.

"If God loves the ones we can't," she said, "then finally maybe we can. All these years I've thought of him in those shadows, with Martha Elizabeth standing there, and his work-sore old hands over his face."

Once the body of Ben Feltner was laid on his bed, the men who had helped Jack to carry him home went quietly out through the kitchen and the back door, as they had come in, muttering or nodding their commiseration in response to Nancy's "Thank you." And Jack stayed. He stayed to be within sight or call of his sister when she needed him, and he stayed to keep his eye on Mat. Their struggle in front of Chatham's store, Jack knew, had changed them both. Because he did not yet know how or how much or if it was complete, it was not yet a change that he was willing, or that he dared, to turn his back on.

Someone was sent to take word to Rebecca Finley, Margaret's mother, and to ask her to come for Bess.

When Rebecca came, Margaret brought Bess down the stairs into the quiet that the women now did their best to disguise. But Bess, who did not know what was wrong, and who tactfully allowed the pretense that nothing was, knew nevertheless that the habits of the house were now broken, and she had heard the quiet that she would never forget.

"Grandma Finley is here to take you home with her," Margaret said, giving her voice the lilt of cheerfulness. "You've been talking about going to stay with her, haven't you?"

And Bess said, dutifully supplying the smile she felt her mother wanted, "Yes."

"We're going to bake some cookies just as soon as we get home," Rebecca said. "Do you want to bake a gingerbread boy?"

"Yes," Bess said.

She removed her hand from her mother's hand and placed it in her grandmother's. They went out the door.

The quiet returned. From then on, though there was much that had to be done and the house stayed full of kin and neighbors coming and going or staying to help, and though by midafternoon women were already bringing food, the house preserved a quiet against all sound. No voice was raised. No door was slammed. Everybody moved as if in consideration, not of each other, but of the quiet itself—as if the quiet denoted some fragile peacefulness in Ben's new sleep that should not be intruded upon.

Jack Beechum was party to that quiet. He made no sound. He said nothing, for his own silence had become wonderful to him and he could not bear to break it. Though Nancy, after the death of their mother, had given Jack much of his upbringing and had been perhaps more his mother than his sister, Ben had never presumed to be a father to him. From the time Jack was eight years old, Ben had been simply his friend—had encouraged, instructed, corrected, helped, and stood by him; had placed a kindly, humorous, forbearing expectation upon him that he could not shed or shirk and had at last lived up to. They had been companions. And yet, through the rest of that day, Jack had his mind more on Mat than Ben.

Jack watched Mat as he would have watched a newborn colt weak on its legs that he had helped to stand, that might continue to stand or might not.

All afternoon Jack did not sit down because Mat did not. Sometimes there were things to do, and they were busy. Space for the coffin had to be made in the living room. Furniture had to be moved. When the time came, the laden coffin had to be moved into place. But, busy or not, Mat was almost constantly moving, as if seeking his place in a world newly made that day, a world still shaking and doubtful underfoot. And Jack both moved with him and stayed apart from him, watching. When they spoke again, they would speak on different terms.

There was a newness in the house, a solemnity, a sort of wariness, a restlessness as of a dog uneasy on the scent of some creature undeniably present but unknown. In its quiet, the house seemed to be straining to accommodate Ben's absence, made undeniable and insistent by the presence of his body lying still under his folded hands.

Jack would come later to his own reckoning with that loss, the horror and the pity of it, and the grief, the awe and gratitude and love and sorrow and regret, when Ben, newly dead and renewing sorrow for others dead before, would wholly occupy his mind in the night, and could give no comfort, and would not leave. But now Jack stayed by Mat and helped as he could.

In the latter part of the afternoon came Della Budge, Miss Della, bearing an iced cake on a stand like a lighted lamp. As she left the kitchen and started for the front door, she laid her eyes on Jack, who was standing in the door between the living room and the hall. She was a large woman, far gone in years. It was a labor for her to walk. She advanced each foot ahead of the other with care, panting, her hand on her hip, rocking from side. She wore many clothes, for her blood was thin and she was easily chilled, and she carried a fan, for sometimes she got too warm. Her little dustcap struggled to stay on top of her head. A tiny pair of spectacles perched awry on her nose. She had a face like a shriveled apple, and the creases at the corners of her mouth were stained with snuff. Once, she had been Jack's teacher. For years they had waged a contest in which she had endeavored to teach him the begats from Abraham to Jesus and he had refused to learn them. He was one of her failures, but she maintained a proprietary interest in him nonetheless. She was the only one left alive who called him "Jackie."

As she came up to him he said, "Hello, Miss Della."

"Well, Jackie," she said, lifting and canting her nose to bring her spectacles to bear upon him, "poor Ben has met his time."

"Yes, mam," Jack said. "One of them things."

"When your time comes you must go, by the hand of man or the stroke of God."

"Yes, mam," Jack said. He was standing with his hands behind him, leaning against the doorjamb.

"It'll come by surprise," she said. "It's a time appointed, but we'll not be notified."

Jack said he knew it. He did know it.

"So we must always be ready," she said. "Pray without ceasing."

"Yes, mam."

"Well, God bless Ben Feltner. He was a good man. God rest his soul."

Jack stepped ahead of her to help her out the door and down the porch steps.

"Why, thank you, Jackie," she said as she set foot at last on the walk.

He stood and watched her going away, walking, it seemed to him, a tottering edge between eternity and time.

Toward evening Margaret laid the table, and the family and several of the neighbor women gathered in the kitchen. Only two or three men had come, and they were sitting in the living room by the coffin. The table was spread with the abundance of food that had been brought in. They were just preparing to sit down when the murmur of voices they had been hearing from the road down in front of the stores seemed to converge and to move in their direction. Those in the kitchen stood and listened a moment, and then Mat started for the front of the house. The others followed him through the hall and out onto the porch.

The sun was down, the light cool and directionless, so that the colors of the foliage and of the houses and storefronts of the town seemed to glow. Chattering swifts circled and swerved above the chimneys. Nothing else moved except the crowd that made its way at an almost formal pace into the yard. The people standing on the porch were as still as everything else, except for Jack Beechum who quietly made his way forward until he stood behind and a little to the left of Mat, who was standing at the top of the steps.

The crowd moved up near the porch and stopped. There was a moment of hesitation while it murmured and jostled inside itself.

"Be quiet, boys," somebody said. "Let Doc do the talking."

They became still, and then Doctor Starns, who stood in the front rank, took a step forward.

"Mat," he said, "we're here as your daddy's friends. We've got word that Thad Coulter's locked up in the jail at Hargrave. We want you to know that we don't like what he did."

Several voices said, "No!" and "Nosir!"

"We know it was a thing done out of meanness. We don't think we can stand for it, or that we ought to, or that we ought to wait on somebody else's opinion about it. He was seen by a large number of witnesses to do what he did."

Somebody said, "That's right!"

"We think it's our business, and we propose to make it our business."

"That's right!" said several voices.

"It's only up to you to say the word, and we'll ride down there tonight and put justice beyond question. We have a rope."

And in the now-silent crowd someone held up a coil of rope, a noose already tied.

The doctor gave a slight bow of his head to Mat and then tipped his hat to Nancy who now stood behind Mat and to his right. And again the crowd murmured and slightly stirred within itself.

For what seemed to Jack a long time, Mat did not speak or move. The crowd grew quiet again, and again they could hear the swifts chittering in the air. Jack's right hand ached to reach out to Mat. It seemed to him again that he felt the earth shaking under his feet, as Mat felt it. But though it shook and though they felt it, Mat now stood resolved and calm upon it. Looking at the back of his head, Jack could still see the boy in him, but the head was up. The voice, when it came, was steady:

"No, gentlemen. I appreciate it. We all do. But I ask you not to do it."

And Jack, who had not sat down since morning, stepped back and sat down.

Nancy, under whose feet the earth was not shaking, if it ever had, stepped up beside her son and took his arm.

She said to the crowd, "I know you are my husband's friends. I thank you. I, too, must ask you not to do as you propose. Mat has asked you; I have asked you; if Ben could, he would ask you. Let us make what peace is left for us to make."

"If you want to," Mat said, "come and be with us. We have food, and you all are welcome."

He had said, in all, six brief sentences. He was not a forward man. This, I think, was the only public speech of his life.

"I can see him yet," my grandmother said, her eyes, full of sudden moisture, again turned to the window. "I wish you could have seen him."

And now, after so many years, perhaps I have. I have sought that moment out, or it has sought me, and I see him standing without prop in the deepening twilight, asking his father's friends to renounce the vengeance that a few hours before he himself had been furious to exact.

This is the man who will be my grandfather—the man who will be the man who was my grandfather. The tenses slur and slide under the pressure of collapsed time. For that moment on the porch is not a now that was but a now that is and will be, inhabiting all the history of Port William that followed and will follow. I know that in the days after his father's death—and after Thad Coulter, concurring in the verdict of his would-be jury in Port William, hung himself in the Hargrave jail and so released Martha Elizabeth from her watch—my grandfather renewed and carried on his friendship with the Coulters: with Thad's widow and daughters, with Dave Coulter and his family, and with another first cousin of Thad's, Marce Catlett, my grandfather on my father's side. And when my father asked leave of the Feltners to marry their daughter Bess, my mother, he was made welcome.

Mat Feltner dealt with Ben's murder by not talking about it and thus keeping it in the past. In his last years, I liked to get him to tell me about the violent old times of the town, the hard drinking and the fighting. And he would oblige me up to a point, enjoying the outrageous old stories himself, I think. But always there would come a time in the midst of the telling when he would become silent, shake his head, lift one hand and let it fall; and I would know— I know better now than I did then—that he had remembered his father's death.

Though Coulters still abound in Port William, no Feltner of the name is left. But the Feltner line continues, joined to the Coulter line, in me, and I am here. I am blood kin to both sides of that moment when Ben Feltner turned to face Thad Coulter in the road and Thad pulled the trigger. The two families, sundered in the ruin of a friendship, were united again first in new friendship and then in marriage. My grandfather made a peace here that has joined many who would otherwise have been divided. I am the child of his forgiveness.

After Mat spoke the second time, inviting them in, the crowd loosened and came apart. Some straggled back down into the town; others, as Mat had asked, came into the house, where their wives already were.

But Jack did not stay with them. As soon as he knew he was free, his thoughts went to other things. His horse had stood a long time, saddled, without water or feed. The evening chores were not yet done. Ruth would be wondering what had happened. In the morning they would come back together, to be of use if they could. And there would be, for Jack as for the others, the long wearing out of grief. But now he could stay no longer.

As soon as the porch was cleared, he retrieved his hat from the hall tree and walked quietly out across the yard under the maples and the descending night. So as not to be waylaid by talk, he walked rapidly down the middle of the road to where he had tied his horse. Lamps had now been lighted in the stores and the houses. As he approached, his horse nickered to him.

"I know it," Jack said.

As soon as the horse felt the rider's weight in the stirrup, he started. Soon the lights and noises of the town were behind them, and there were only a few stars, a low red streak in the west, and the horse's eager footfalls on the road.

Guides to Reflection

1. In the opening sentence of "Pray without Ceasing," the narrator, Andy Catlett, catches himself using the past tense ("was") in reference to his grandfather who, he realizes anew, is dead. Yet because the "past is present also," Mat Feltner is still very much with his family, as the retelling of his life will go on to demonstrate. How does the narrator's meditation on time at the beginning of the story prepare us to understand it?

2. Andy's grandmother begins her account by saying, "If it hadn't been for Jack Beechum, Mat *would* have killed him" *(Reader, 44)*. This alerts us to the importance of Jack and of the particular moment when, in a "desperate embrace," he prevented Mat from wrecking vengeance on Thad Coulter. Berry writes, "Jack felt that his arms would pull apart at the joints. He ached afterward. Something went out of him that day, and he was not the same again. And what went out of Jack came into Mat" *(Reader, 58)*. Comment on the significance of this exchange between the two men.

3. The title of the story comes from the Bible (1 Thessalonians 5:17) and is introduced into the story by Della Budge during a conversation with Jack Beechum *(Reader, 69)*. How is the verse used at this moment in the text and what is its larger relevance to the story? Why might Berry have chosen it for a title?

4. Comment on the character Mary Elizabeth Coulter. We know very little about her thoughts and feelings. Because she is largely silent, we know her only through her actions. What role does she play in the story? What do you make of the fact that, in her old age, she is said to be a woman "always near to smiling, sometimes to laughter" *(Reader, 65)?*

5. The recovery of the past in "Pray without Ceasing" comes as the result of Andy Catlett's questioning. Although the story of his great-grandfather's murder seems to have nothing to do with him, it comes in the end to reveal his own identity and to suggest how "the past is present" in each of us. How is the story's narrator important rather than incidental to the narrative?

6. Discuss the following observation about the mysterious nature of divine love, not only in terms of Berry's story but with regard to your own experience: "People sometimes talk of God's love as if it's a pleasant thing. But it is terrible, in a way. Think of all it includes. It included Thad Coulter, drunk and mean and foolish, before he killed Mr. Feltner, and it included him afterwards" *(Reader, 66).*

4

Oscar Hijuelos

Since his first novel, *Our House in the Last World,* was published in 1983, Oscar Hijuelos has received much praise and many awards, including the Pulitzer Prize for *The Mambo Kings Play Songs of Love* (1989). Critics admire the expansiveness and the moral seriousness of his work. One reviewer, commenting on *The Fourteen Sisters of Emilio Montez O'Brien* (1993), said: "Once in a great while a novelist emerges who is remarkable not for the particulars of his prose but for the breadth of his soul, the depth of his humanity, and for the precision of his gauge on the rising sensibilities of his time.... Oscar Hijuelos is one of these."[1] Readers have found this same breadth and depth in Hijuelos's more recent novels, *Mr. Ives' Christmas* (1995) and *Empress of the Splendid Season* (1999).

Born in New York City in 1951 of Cuban immigrants, Hijuelos has lived and worked on the Upper West Side of Manhattan for most of his life. He holds degrees from City College of New York. Before his first novel was published, he worked in advertising for a number of years. All of his novels, except *Fourteen Sisters,* are set in the Upper West Side, and all concern Cuban-Americans, many of whom long for their old world of pre-Castro Cuba while they struggle to adjust to their new world in the United States. Most of his central characters, immigrants working hard to establish themselves, nevertheless remain in the lower class. Hijuelos's stories show great sensitivity for these characters who live on the edges of society. They work long hours for low wages, worry about the safety of their children, and take on extra jobs to pay bills if a family member falls ill.

While severely limited by the economic realities of their lives, Hijuelos's characters are not circumscribed in other ways. Many are musicians, painters, or poets in the time they can spare from their day jobs. While they are often discouraged or frightened by their circumstances, they find ways to escape or overcome them in their art.

Hijuelos's characters are often religious. Among the many characters in his novels Hijuelos presents various kinds of religious experience and belief, but religious concerns and questions form a leitmotif throughout all the novels. Religion is as much a part of the worlds Hijuelos portrays as love, work, friendship, and money.

Because of the sweeping scope of Hijuelos's novels, reviewers often compare them to novels by Gabriel Garcia Marquez and Charles Dickens. Like them, Hijuelos writes long novels that span decades, tracing the lives of the central characters. The novels include many minor characters whose lives raise issues of importance to the protagonists, and the novels place their characters in particular social and historical contexts that the novelists explore in depth.

The comparison of Hijuelos to Dickens is particularly apt because both writers create worlds imbued with a moral vision. In *Mr. Ives' Christmas* Hijuelos specifically recalls Dickens' *A Christmas Carol.* Early in the novel, the reader learns that not only is Dickens the favorite author of the central character, Edward Ives, but Ives inherits and treasures some copies of first editions of Dickens' work. Ives' son, Robert, reads and rereads the novel. Edward's wife, Annie, teaches *A Christmas Carol* to her high school class, praising Dickens' concern for the poor and pointing out the story's moral: "There can be no greater reward than goodness to your fellow man" *(Reader 82).*

Mr. Ives' Christmas differs from Dickens' work because it has not only a moral framework for its story, but an explicitly religious one as well. While religious questions echo throughout Hijuelos's work, religion plays a particularly crucial role in *Mr. Ives' Christmas,* defining the central foci of the entire novel. Hijuelos has said that the genesis of the novel was in a conversation he once had with a philosophy professor who judged him to be "a moron for believing in God."[2] Throughout the novel, Mr. Ives asks himself again and again if his religious beliefs make sense, or if, in a world of violence and sorrow, only morons believe in God.

The test of Mr. Ives' faith occurs in the central section of the novel, a part entitled "Christmas 1967." Here Hijuelos presents the event that his narrator, in the first pages of the book, has told readers will happen. Ives' son Robert, 17 years old and about to enter a seminary to prepare for the priesthood, is shot and killed as he leaves choir practice just before Christmas 1967. The boy who shoots Robert does so on a whim, because he does not like the way Robert smiles. The killing severely tests the faith of Mr. Ives, who has been a devout Catholic all his life and a kind and good presence in his Manhattan neighborhood. An advertising executive, he volunteers time to various service organizations in his multiracial neighborhood where people of all economic classes live. He is a faithful friend to people of various ethnic backgrounds. Ives' religious faith not only inspires him to do good deeds, but grows as he has a mystical experience one day, and as he discusses with Robert his sense of call to the priesthood.

The random killing of Ives' son is a senseless evil act that happens to a good person, Robert, and his family. The questions that absorb Ives throughout the rest of the novel are those that absorb others who suffer: Why does God allow evil things to happen, especially to good, faithful people? What might forgiveness mean after such an evil act? Does it make any sense to have religious faith after experiencing such evil?

Ives' grief after "Christmas 1967" fills many long years. In the remaining sections of the novel, Hijuelos tells both of Ives' continuing struggle to remain faithful despite his doubt and despair and of Ives' painstaking journey to forgiveness for the belatedly repentant murderer. The novel closes with two visions, one in which Ives encounters his son, who offers him a baptism-like renewal, and the second, a reverie Ives has in church in which he imagines Jesus coming down off the cross to bless and redeem him.

The resolution Ives achieves at the novel's end is hard won. Ives' faith is not an easy, sentimental one. The test Ives faces in "Christmas 1967" is a severe, Job-like test. It lies at the center of what the reviewer in the *New York Times* praised as "the deepest and the best"[3] of Hijuelos's novels and what the novelist Larry Woiwode has called "one of the high points in the last decade of American fiction."[4] Hijuelos's story of *Mr. Ives' Christmas* is an absorbing, haunting novel of a life of faith.

Paula J. Carlson

Notes

1. *Washington Post Book World* (14 March 1993): 1.
2. Sara Mosle, "Father and Son," *New Yorker* (21 & 28 August 1995): 128.
3. Miles, Jack, "The Ghost of a Christmas Past," *New York Times Book Review* (3 Dec. 1995): 9.
4. Larry Woiwode, "When Christmas Dies," *Books and Culture* (May/June 1996): 8.

Christmas 1967

The Tree Party

It was a Tuesday evening, the week before Christmas 1967, and Mr. Ives and his children had come back from Amsterdam Avenue and 119th Street, where the local kids sold trees outside a stationery store called "Jack's." As in previous years, Ives bought a balsam fir, its spectacular forest smell and pagan benevolence filling not just the living room but all the rooms of the apartment, called by the local kids a "house" (as in "You going to your house, Tommy?"). They put up a large wreath on the front door, smaller wreaths and strings of lights in the windows, blinking at all the other windows with their wreaths and lights, even those windows from which came loud, raucous, and tinny Latin music at night.

Earlier in the day Ives had walked over from the office to Ninth Avenue during lunchtime, to buy boxes of Italian cold cuts and pastries, and these were set out on a table as a buffet. Around eight some friends came over: Arnie, a bachelor grocery counterman, whom they felt sorry for; their down-the-hall neighbors, the Chevaliers, a Haitian family; and one of Annie's schoolteacher friends, a nice lady named Esther, past forty and unmarried, whom they hoped to fix up with Arnie. Then there were some of the neighborhood kids, friends of their children, who, each year, came to devour the first-rate food and to help decorate the tree. Finally, the bell would ring again, and Ramirez and his wife and kids would be at the door with boxes of pastries and several bottles of Spanish wine or chilled nickel-refund bottles of Rheingold beer, dark brown glass sweating. Ives would put some Perry Como or Bing Crosby on the big RCA console with the twenty-one-inch black-and-white TV, radio, and phonograph that his boss had given him as an extra-special bonus one year, and the tree-decorating party would begin, the adults chatting on the couch, eating, everyone smoking cigarettes and watching kids at work.

They decorated the tree with sets of blue, red, yellow, and green lights that resembled medicine droppers or dragonflies, bubbles undulating through their shifting liquid centers; the kind of lights whose wires often overheated and started many a fire in tenement apartments all over the city. They put up strings of lights with angel sconces and holly-colored beads. There were ornaments from the closet, snow-sprayed and clumped with strands of last year's tinsel clinging to them. Several were holdovers from Ives' Brooklyn childhood, battered, flaking, and chipped, but royally old and precious (along with different pieces of a crèche set) and some had come from Annie's home. And there were the ornaments Ives and Annie bought in antique shops and street markets, and some ceramic *putti* that they had found in a small shop off La Via di Penitenza, near the Vatican, on a rainy afternoon in Rome, during their trip to Italy years before.

Now, Ives watched one year turning into another and had already began to miss Robert's and Caroline's childhood, perhaps more than they did themselves. As he sat on the couch with his adult friends, half listening while Ramirez spoke about the changes that had taken place in Cuba, to which he'd hoped to one day retire, Ives became ever more nostalgic. Not so long ago his children were infants and he and Annie had lived to make their Christmases happy. He recalled his pleasures at giving his children just what they wanted at Christmas, *nearly* spoiling them, and nearly so because even though he would have done anything to make them happy, he and Annie had seen to it that they earned their way in the world. Robert had passed many of the mornings of his youth, before going off to school, delivering newspapers or working for a neighborhood laundry service, watching the shop while the boss made his runs. In the late afternoons when he was not studying, he often went to work in a pharmacy on Broadway. Odd jobs here and there, and his duties as a student, altar boy, and choir tenor, had kept him felicitously busy. And Caroline helped an old woman in the building, Mrs. Myers, to keep her apartment clean, occasionally baby-sat and worked behind the counter of Party Cake bakery. She was all of thirteen.

But he made it a point of telling his son, "Never take your good looks or coloring as something better." Although many of his son's classmates at Corpus and later high school were black and Spanish-speaking kids, Ives went a step further and he encouraged his quiet son to join a Harlem baseball league. For several years Robert had the distinction of being the only white boy, playing left field, on a softball team called the Harlem Ravens, which made it into third and fourth place in the city two years running. He eventually had to quit because he was always getting jumped and coming home covered with bruises and with other injuries, about which he never complained but which broke his parents' hearts and tested Ives' convictions.

That evening passed festively enough. The tree had been decorated with great aplomb and by ten-thirty everyone had left and the children were in bed. Buoyed by the companionship of his friends and family, Ives consumed a few more drinks than usual. In the dark of the living room, with only the tree lights on and Bach playing on the hi-fi, Ives and Annie had remained on the couch, relaxing. He would remember certain things about that gathering. That Arnie had seemed jittery about Esther, but had gotten along well with her anyway; that Ramirez and Carmen had been in especially good spirits. Ramirez had talked about one day opening a restaurant in midtown, serving good Cuban cuisine, and he had told Ives that he had better save his money and could count on becoming a partner. He would recall being ever aware of Pablo's interest in Caroline, as they sat in a corner talking quietly about the Beatles, and how later they stood before the bookcases where Pablo noticed the addition of several Robert Lewis Stevenson novels and *The Plumed Serpent* by D. H. Lawrence. That his son and daughter had kissed him goodnight. Before leaving for his bedroom, Robert had, in his sunny way, reminded them that he had choir practice scheduled at the Church of the Ascension the next day at four.

"We'll be singing from a program of Praetorious and Bach," he said.

At around eleven that night, a predicted snowfall had come. He and Annie looked out about midnight before pulling the plug on the tree lights and going to bed, and mutually agreed how peaceful and clean the streets of New York seemed in such weather.

Things Were Not Well with the Boss

The next day, Ives was in the office by eight-forty-five, the last business meeting of the year before the Christmas holidays, with various art directors and executives, scheduled for half past nine. Afterward there would be a company luncheon, and then the office would close for a pleasantly long weekend at three, and the parties, held here and there at different agencies and suppliers, would begin. There was always work to be done, but aside from the billing and accounting departments, the agency had in effect closed down a few days before. Gifts—bottles of booze, boxes of candies, and other items— circulated around, the high point coming when Mr. Mannis himself, jovial and friendly, made the rounds, robustly shook each employee's hand, and gave out the Christmas bonus, which usually consisted of two or three weeks' pay. His employees were used to seeing a virile and handsome man in his midfifties, but this year, his manner was rather downcast and despondent, an intense sorrow about him, even when he, a thoughtful employer, tried to seem cheerful, given the holiday. A few months before, his nineteen-year-old son had lost both his legs in Saigon, and since then he had been in a mood that would later mirror Ives' own. His boy would die in transport on his way to Australia.

Mannis had given out the bonuses early that morning, and when he had come into Ives' office, he dallied for a moment over some of the pamphlets Ives had picked up at a spiritist lecture. One of them, entitled *Will There Be a Tomorrow?* with its cover of a soul in flight through the cosmos, seemed to have intrigued Mr. Mannis, and when Ives asked, "Would you like to take that with you?" he told him, "Thank you, Ed. Do you mind?"

And he'd tapped Ives' shoulder thoughtfully and, maintaining his composure, had marched out of the office, shoulders back, chest out, a look of devastation upon his face.

Teaching High School

Just as the agency meeting was beginning, Annie MacGuire was standing in the front of a public high school classroom in Upper Manhattan. She had agreed to help out a friend by substituting for her that morning, and although she usually had a strong sense of control about these kinds of situations, this particular group of kids were about as badly behaved as any she had ever encountered. She walked in with a copy of Dylan Thomas' *A Child's Christmas in Wales,* which, given the season, she thought might be appropriate to read aloud. But no sooner had she introduced herself and begun than a shouting match between two students over a pack of cigarettes started, each calling the other a motherfucker and a liar. Just a few years before she would have interceded. She had friends, female teachers, who'd been spit at, had been "flashed," had their teeth knocked out by students they'd tried to discipline, had cigarette butts put out in their hair, friends who had been raped under stairwells. She herself had watched a young man expose himself and slap the table to draw attention to himself, had seen young girls making out wildly, and had once shouted at a young woman busily masturbating her male friend in the back of a class. The very worst jobs always started out badly, with the kids smoking and carrying on and throwing things around, spitting at each other and exuding such menace that she'd wish she were a man, or teaching in some distant and beautiful place that perhaps only existed in her mind, a quaint country school in England in 1904.

She sometimes gave a talk about what hard work would get someone, and the kids either responded by clapping or they shouted insults, the most common being, "Oh yeah, if education is so good for you, then what are you doing here?" Because to some of them being *there* was the worst thing in the world. And sometimes the kids laughed at her and cursed, or they stared at her blankly and she'd realized that many of them did not speak or understand English.

Honor classes were her favorite, because faced with attentive students she could give talks about writers like Lawrence or Charles Dickens, the latter a favorite of hers to teach. She would point out to the poorest kids that not all writers were upper-class fops, as was their impression. Dickens came from humble stock, as did Lawrence. She would tell them about how Charles Dickens had the greatest sympathy for the poor because he had known suffering himself: his father had gone to the poorhouse and died young, and he himself had worked as a kid in a "blacking house," the deprivations of that time something he would never forget. Dickens, she said, had lived for his fame and wrote out of a need for acceptance, but he had also deeply believed that a man's life's work might bring about social change.

She liked to talk about the circumstances of his most famous story, *A Christmas Carol.* Dickens was in the habit of taking very long walks through the city of London at night, she would say, and had seen so many poor children working in sweatshops and starving in the streets that he had been moved to write a story about a rich man who has a change of heart toward the poor. And if she had the time, she would read parts of it aloud, and always reiterated that tale's moral: *There can be no greater reward than goodness to your fellow man.*

"He had a kind heart," she said to one class in East Harlem. "He believed that only a heartless society would leave its unfortunate poor to its sad fortune."

And a kid with a coy expression raised his hand and asked: "And what country did this man live in?"

Later, there had been an afternoon assembly and the special speaker had been the writer Piri Thomas, the heart of whose message to the kids had been, "It's cool to hang out, but there comes a point when if you want to get out of the barrio you can't hang out on the stoop anymore," advice met mainly by jeers and boos. She'd remembered that the next morning, while discussing his talk with a different class, her defense of Piri Thomas' sentiment was met with derision. As she thought of her own high ideals, their reaction had brought her to tears: she left the classroom and had fled into the faculty ladies' room, where she stood over a sink crying her eyes out for half an hour, until she realized why she had taken it so hard: something in the expressions of those students reminded her of her own brothers and other members of her family who used to laugh and give her a hard time just because she wanted to escape a world of ignorance. It struck her just then that there was no escape, with or without a Dickens or a Piri Thomas in the world, that ignorance just went on and on and on.

The Nature of Those Parties

Some years it was Le Pavilion or the Chambord or the Waldorf-Astoria or the Oyster Bar in Grand Central or Keens Chophouse or the Biltmore Men's Bar, but that December the agency held its Christmas party-luncheon at a Cattleman steak house on Lexington Avenue. By two-thirty in the afternoon a number of employees, who had earlier stormed the open bar and drunk champagne and wine with the buffet lunch as they toasted the coming holiday, were hanging around a cocktail pianist, arms locked around each other's waists like college protesters, swaying, smoking cigarettes, drinking, and singing Christmas carols.

Packed in that room, a dense crowd of employees and invited friends and associates; among them Mr. Ives, who spent much of his time talking with one of the account execs, a certain Mr. Freeman, with whom he went back many years, a ruddy-faced, red-haired old-time advertising man, who dressed like a college professor in tweed suits and red-dotted bow ties. Ever civil, they mainly talked about their families, and tended toward great silences while taking in the proceedings with amused expressions.

Ives and Freeman were two of the more respectable higher-ups. "Family men," whom the slightly looped secretaries tended to praise to death at these parties, for their gentlemanly natures and fidelity to their wives. With thirty-nine years at the agency between them (seventeen for Ives and twenty-two for Freeman, who had started at the agency just after graduating from Yale in 1945), they, in their forties, represented something of the composed and more refined "old guard." Over the years they had been privy to the not-so-private craziness induced by too much holiday drinking. One could go hopping from party to party, drinking all day, if one liked. Many did. For the young unmarried—and married—wolves, who lurked about, Christmas drinking afforded the the best opportunity to whisk a young "lamb" off to bed. The previous year one of the secretaries, drinking too much, had been goaded by a crowd, men and women, into taking off her clothes. She had stripped down to her brassiere and began to expose one of her large moon-shaped breasts, when Ives, feeling morally indignant, marched over and, like an angry, concerned father, pulled her down from the table, saying: "Come on, child, you don't know what you're doing." And to the others he'd chided, "My God, are you crazy?" At that same gathering, a young Italian secretary, who was engaged to be married in the New Year, fell momentarily in love with a handsome account executive from Y & R, and hid away for hours in a corner drinking stingers and kissing him. Afterward, she went off with him to a bar, and that was all, until, three days later, she woke up naked on a beach in Puerto Rico, without a memory of how she had gotten there.

Forty-five years old, Ives was considered well into midcareer, and was already thinking about retiring in another ten years or so; there was a grind about the job that was slowly wearing him down, even if he no longer put in the kind of hours he had when he was in his late twenties and early thirties. That is, he had "spent" a certain amount of his ambition and drive for the agency, proving himself, and now, as with others like Freeman, he'd hoped to eventually reap the benefits: buy a vacation home in the country, travel, paint, look after his children. And grandchildren if Caroline married and started her own family.

Proud of what he had done to change the company, as with the Spanish division, he now mainly supervised and okayed artwork to which he could not particularly relate, his blue-penciled initials and corrections appearing in the margins of work produced by the newer, younger artists, who were in touch with the latest fashions. Ives, in his middle age, had spied the sixties from afar, and while he knew about the Beatles and Carnaby Street and Andy Warhol from magazines and the news and *The Ed Sullivan Show,* in his mind what advertising should look and feel like still had to do with the emerging postwar America of the Eisenhower years. While his own style of illustration went by the wayside, a new kind of "free-form" creativity started to show up in advertising art—a style that Ives could not, nor wanted to, adopt. As too conservative an artist to offer anything fresh, Ives might have had reason to fear for his job had Mannis been a different kind of employer. From his office, he watched the company slowly change. They'd even hired several young black college graduates as account reps and there was a buzz regarding the possible hiring of a woman to run promotion. Those were changes that he liked, but, just the same, Ives had moments in the office when the sense that he had wasted himself creatively would come over him, and he would feel nostalgia for his younger days, when he had fantasies about the creative life. On the other hand, he was not Michelangelo and knew it, and would feel a kind of inward gratitude toward his own resources and toward God, and had already started to daydream about other options—syndicated comic strips, children's books, and perhaps paintings themselves.

He refused to give in, to become something that he was not, like those garment-district executives who were his age and older and had grown their hair long and had taken to wearing Nehru jackets and love beads (Ives thought, to convince themselves that they were younger or to get young women). He still wore suits or blazers and put on a tie and a hat, got his hair cut once every two weeks at Juanito's on 123rd and Broadway, caring less what the young hip executives in the office thought, as if a fashion statement, a uniform, could really define an identity or inward soul.

That year he and Freeman talked about how the kids were doing. He had two boys in college and a third about to graduate from high school the coming spring, all red-haired and freckle-faced. Once they were all out of the house he was going to buy a place down in Palm Beach, where he hoped to live the life of a gentleman. Ives told him, a fellow Catholic, the news that his son had decided to attend a seminary.

"Are you happy about that?" Freeman had asked.

"Yes, how could I not be?"

While standing there they were aware, and sadly so, of certain absences. Not of the young cocky, job-hopping execs who barely stayed a year and left, or some of the old-timers like Mr. Palucci, a big-billboard man who had retired, nor of the secretaries or file clerks who came and went, pleasantly enough, but of several executives, one of them not yet forty, a certain Mr. Gianni. He had run the television division and was so tense that just standing next to him one could feel his aggravations. He had died during a lunchtime indoor tennis match at the New York Racquet Club in Grand Central Terminal, a few months before. There had been Saul Zimmerman, another art director, who seemed particularly obsessed about reading the *New York Times* obituaries with his morning coffee, and each Christmas always commented, "My God, I can't believe how quickly all this time is going." He had died from cancer that past spring, not yet fifty-two.

They toasted those departed friends and their fellow workers who had good fortune. Like a certain Mr. Shinn, who had won five thousand dollars earlier that year in New York State's first "scratch away" lottery, or Miss Feingold, now Mrs. Mallon, down from Coop City in the Bronx to show off her twin three-year-old daughters, telling them, when she introduced Mr. Ives, "See, this is the man Mommy was stuck in the elevator with." They greeted one of the mafia printers, who wore four diamond rings on his hand and told everybody, *"Buona festa!"* And there was the oldest employee at the agency, a Mr. Myers from the mailroom, going on about some past glory. (He'd started out with another agency as a messenger back in the late 1920s and had a memory for odd New York events, like walking down Madison Avenue making a delivery the morning that a B-25 bomber collided with the Empire State Building.)

Eventually one of the senior vice presidents, Mr. Crane, Mannis' right-hand man, gave a speech on the boss's behalf; Mr. Mannis, his spirits low, had left the office shortly after noon and was preparing to go off to London with his wife that evening to spend a week in the chilling English cold, catching East End theater shows. In any event, through Mr. Crane he thanked his employees and wished them the best for the coming year. Then a raffle was held, many small gifts handed out by an actor playing Santa Claus, the grand prize a week in the Virgin Islands. Gradually the crowd started to drift off, to attend other affairs, or to go home, or to meet up, as Ives did with

Annie, with their spouses. She arrived shortly after three, so that they could get in some shopping.

With the Immortal Mr. Frankie of Macy's

So, Ives would remember, he and Annie had dallied at the office party just long enough for her to wolf down a quick plate of food, to say hello to some of his fellow employees, before heading downtown along Fifth Avenue. They passed the remainder of the afternoon making their way through crowds and going in and out of department stores, before ending up in Macy's.

Roaming through the aisles, Ives had picked up some half-dozen ties and wallets for certain male friends, a scarf for his brother, and a nice French hat for his sister Kate. That year he had decided on buying Robert a good watch and prevailed upon an overwhelmed saleswoman to pull some twenty watches out of a case, before he settled on a black-banded gold Hamilton with Roman numerals, suitable, Ives had thought, for a young man headed to a seminary.

Finished with their shopping and on their way out, Ives had asked one of the old security guards if a certain Mr. Frankie happened to be around. For three years, from 1938 to 1941, Ives had worked alongside him each Christmas season, painting backdrops and helping to set up mechanical displays in Macy's windows. As it happened, they found Mr. Frankie on the Sixth Avenue side of the store, in a cluttered workshop off one of the hidden stockrooms, trying to repair a female automaton. A slender and slight man with delicate features and the smallest hands, Mr. Frankie seemed nearly doll-like himself. His hair, dyed to a nearly golden color and rippling like the sea, appeared stiff, as if from lacquer; seeing him, Ives remembered that even on the windiest nights Mr. Frankie's hair never moved. Of a rather coquettish demeanor, as was typical of window dressers and display artists, and with a perpetual tan, Mr. Frankie behaved around Ives as would a beloved eccentric uncle, wrapping his arms around him and giving Ives a kiss on the neck.

Putting aside his work, he sat his guests down, made them hot rum toddies, before filling them in on the events of his recent life. Ives would remember feeling especially amused and a little confounded by him that evening: while Ives himself had aged more than twenty years since they last worked together in 1947, Mr. Frankie, ever delicate and small, in a light blue V-neck cashmere sweater, white trousers, and violet scarf around his neck, seemed not to have aged a single hour.

A Malaise

Earlier Caroline and her brother had gone to a Sam Goody's in their mother and father's old neighborhood, to Christmas shop. Afterward, they took the subway back, and while Robert went to his choir practice at four, Caroline had gotten off at 116th Street. But instead of going home to Claremont, she had met a friend and they had taken a bus down to Eighty-fifth Street and walked over to Central Park West to a boy's apartment. His name was Kirk and he was a fifteen-year-old prep-school kid who acted as if he had lost his virginity; he had long hair, bangs that fell over his brow, and a chiseled pretty-boy face, with high cheekbones, clear blue eyes, dimpled chin, the kind poor kids love to smash up, and he was tall and a sharp dresser. His father was a professor at Columbia, and she had met him at a square dance over at the Horace Mann School on 120th Street one Sunday afternoon. She had gone there at the suggestion of a friend, who thought she might get an idea of what hipper, more refined, and worldly boys were like. That translated into English as non-poor, non-working-class-boys. At that dance he noticed the way that Caroline, smitten by his appearance, had looked at him, and thinking her older, as she rarely smiled, he had called her friend and invited them over for some "fun."

His parents were not at home, and he and his friend set up a table with Coca-Cola and rum and ice and potato chips. Because he had talked to Caroline long enough to ascertain that she liked groups like the Beatles and the Zombies, as opposed to groups like the Rolling Stones, he put these albums on a turntable, offered her hand-rolled cigarettes made out of tobacco, and then held out a pipe filled with burning marijuana. She took a few puffs, coughed and rolled back onto the couch, feeling slightly nauseated: when she got up and looked in a mirror she thought she had never seen anything so funny or ugly or homely in her life. Then she dallied in a corner for a long time before joining the party again. She was wearing a brown skirt and brown turtleneck sweater with a black belt, high black boots, fishnet stockings, and a Portuguese mariner's cap, made popular by the folksingers she had seen walking on the streets during her excursions with her father and brother to the bookshops of Greenwich Village.

They had gotten there about a quarter to five, and she had to be home at seven. But when she checked the time again it was twenty to the hour. That's when Kirk brought out a paper bag and filled it with the contents of a thirty-cent tube of DuPont model glue. Burying his nose in the opening, he suddenly flew back as if someone had smacked him in the head with a two-by-four, laughing wildly. Then he gave her a whiff and she found herself circling overhead, her thoughts whipping along, propelled by the chemicals, the feeling of strangeness multiplying when he clicked off the light and lit a candle, and then brought her out of that dark blue and black atmosphere into reality. She opened her eyes and realized that he had his hand up her skirt and that the crawling sensations inside her were caused by the clumsy groping of several of his fingers, and while one part of her seemed interested and flattered and excited, another part of her disliked every last bit of what was happening. And she would remember how, at about seven-fifteen or so, as she had stood up and pulled down her skirt and looked for the light, a sensation of utter and complete sadness abruptly rushed into her, lingering there and then suddenly vanishing.

Thinking that it had to do with sinning, she quickly made her way out of that apartment, leaving her friend behind, rushing across Columbus Avenue to catch an Amsterdam bus uptown, her stomach and heart in knots. Happy and relieved to be getting home, she was mainly concerned that her father might have started to worry about her. She leaned her face against the window and noticed a battery of police cars and ambulances around 107th Street, their red lights flashing, building facades flickering on and off like neon signs, and she hoped that nothing bad had happened. Her thoughts focused instead on how she had been stupid and allowed herself to get carried away by a handsome face, and that the marijuana had not sat well with her, that the glue had a depressing aftereffect, even if it had been exciting to embark upon an adventure.

On Claremont

Leaving Macy's, they spent an hour walking uptown and lingered by the Rockefeller Center ice-skating rink, on the promenade, directly across from the bronze statue of Prometheus reclining, the great tree, a Maine pine, some fifty feet high and as wide as a house, covered with thousands of lights, towering cheerfully over the scene. Down below, a hundred skaters, of all ages, circled the ice, some gracefully as professionals, others clumsily, their faces and twisting bodies in colored caps and suits, vivid in the surrounding floodlights. Leaning against the railing, Annie and Ives were caught up, as were so many others, by the romance of the setting, and, ever so happy, held each other tightly, nudging one another with their chilled noses and stealing kisses, until laughing, she said, "Oh, Eddie, you make me feel like a kid again."

As they happily walked to the subway, they were looking forward to spending a lot of time together at home during the holiday, in the company of family and friends. Ives and Annie had stopped to peer into a window display of French linen when, just like that, a terrible darkness entered them, and they could not move and stood looking at one another stupidly, on the crowded and busy sidewalk.

Not Enough Wine or Scotch

They were in one of those states that come from having had enough to drink but not enough to ward off an early hangover, and as they made their way from the 116th Street station toward Claremont, Ives began to suffer from a headache and was thinking that he would have a nice glass of scotch at home and take a couple of aspirins. Maybe they would order takeout from the Chinese joint on 124th, or go to the local bar, Malloy's, whose big sign he himself had designed and painted, where they had good tap beer and hamburgers rated among the best in the city, Ives in the mood for its unsavory atmosphere every so often. But as Ives and Annie passed 120th Street and were approaching their building, they could see people milling about in front of their stoop—dozens of their neighbors, among them Ramirez and his son, who came solemnly toward them, Ramirez' face a mask of grief. Two police cars were parked in front. The first thing Ives thought was that something had happened to Caroline: she was getting strong-headed lately and might have gone off to the park by herself, which he had warned her about a hundred times, but soon he saw her on the stoop, her head buried against Carmen Ramirez' arms. And then he saw Mr. Ramirez' stony face, eyes wide open: with Ives' forearm in his grip, he squeezed it more tightly than it had ever been squeezed before, and he said: *"Hermano."* And shortly, as Annie stood atop the steps with her daughter, shopping bags by her side, Ives found himself walking between two plainclothes police officers. Ramirez followed behind them and got into the front seat of an unmarked police car, sitting beside one of the officers. Then, leaving Caroline with Mrs. Ramirez, Annie got into the back beside her husband.

As the automobile pulled away from the curb, another green-and-white police car followed. Ives and Annie did not say a word and just watched the streets and lights flashing by as they made their way along Tiemann to 123rd, and then uptown again. A train pulled into the elevated station and his wife, nestling her head against his shoulder, sighed. He noticed that in a first-floor window on Broadway a family had put up a lovely display of the Holy Mother posed in a Christmas setting, with a wreath of red and pink and light blue electric lights blinking crazily around her, and that she was flanked by two oversized electric candles, which gave off a tremendous pink light, the kind of gaudy but pleasing display one generally found in the poorer parts of the city.

Then the cop behind the wheel offered each a cigarette, and Ives said rather matter-of-factly, "No thanks, but that brand is one of my company's biggest advertisers."

In the back of that police car, he remembered a four-color ad he had drawn one Christmas, about 1954–1955, for a toy company: in it, a young sleepy-eyed boy, newly awakened on Christmas morning, stands before a richly decorated tree, gasping with delight over an electric train set, an illustration he had based on his son. The boy looked just like Robert, and Ives could see him crawling around the floor of their old apartment on Fiftieth Street and exploring the lowest boughs of the Christmas tree, strands of tinsel, lights and ornaments glowing like majestic stars above him; his son reaching up, his son's fine lips slightly parted, heavy-lidded eyes wide.

And then Ives blinked and found himself standing on the sidewalk beside his wife, across the street from the Church of the Ascension. On the pavement, just by his feet, was a large piece of canvas, and under it a body, stretched out. Then the officer lifted off the canvas and shined a flashlight onto the face to reveal the shocked and bewildered expression of his son.

What a Cop Handed Ives

One of the kids would say that Robert had showed up in generally good spirits around a quarter after four, a little late, and that they joked about the prospect of getting hired to record the theme song to a cartoon show about outer-space hounds from Japan in the new year, work that Ives had gotten them through a connection; that he walked in with a Sam Goody's shopping bag as well as another bag filled with different items, mainly paperback books. Dressed too lightly for the cool day, he had worn a long black-hooded raincoat and a cap that he didn't like because it messed up his fine dark hair, brown penny loafers and galoshes, a Cardinal Spellman High School senior ring. During the break he sat around with a couple of his friends in the choir room, showing them the 33rpm records he had bought as Christmas presents that afternoon, about fifteen albums in all.

The records were in a Sam Goody's shopping bag, which a police officer had retrieved from the scene. He handed it over to Mr. Ives, saying, "I guess these were his." In his shock Ives stood under a street lamp going over his son's purchases: he'd bought albums by Thelonius Monk, Art Blakey, and the Jazz Messengers, and John Coltrane for his mother; a Dixieland recording and a Nonesuch anthology of Gregorian chant for his father. There were recordings by the Dave Clark Five, the Young Rascals, and the Beatles for Caroline. A Temptations record for an old pal, Richie, a Golden Oldies anthology for Pablo. He had bought a recording of the Goldberg Variations by Bach for his choirmaster at Corpus, and a Mass by Palestrina for his choirmaster at Ascension. He had bought Perry Como and Rosemary Clooney albums for his Aunt Kate.

God Has Called Him to Heaven

His murderer took ten dollars from the other boy and walked over to Amsterdam Avenue, not one hundred yards away, calmly hailed a gypsy cab, and went up to 136th Street and Broadway, to a block that once was largely Irish but that had become, over the past few years, mainly Puerto Rican and black.

When a five-hundred-dollar reward for any information regarding the crime was offered, the taxi driver, a Dominican who had not liked the boy's arrogance, decided to call the cops. He told them where he had picked up the kid, where he had dropped him off, and how, incidentally, he had been stiffed on his two-dollar fare. The boy was a mulatto, about five feet seven inches in height, solidly built, maybe 180 pounds, with a short haircut, mustache, about fourteen to fifteen years old. He was wearing a striped turtleneck sweater, an army jacket with a 1st Cavalry patch sewn onto the shoulder, and a woolen cap. The cops found him the next day.

He was so arrogant and cocksure that he had not bothered to hide or even to change his clothing and, in fact, had been bragging to his friends in the neighborhood about having popped "a rich white boy," and showed off his .22-caliber pistol, which he carried around in a paper bag and occasionally fired at night, leaving holes in apartment-house windows. Even though many a street below 125th Street was filled with tenements and junkies, he had the fantasy that rich people lived around there. The proximity of Columbia University gave that neighborhood, which had more than its share of problems, the allure, in his mind, of Park Avenue, even when some strips, say Amsterdam Avenue, running from 120th all the way down to the Nineties were pretty much working class or poor. There were projects on 125th Street, stretching from Broadway way east of Madison Avenue, and a row of New York City high-rise projects on the east side of Amsterdam to about 123rd, where the neighborhood, turning left, headed into the center of Harlem.

The cops found him in his aunt's second-floor apartment, sitting on her plastic-covered living-room couch, reading *Thor, the Thunder God* and *Fantastic Four* comic books, which he bought with part of the ten dollars. With a shrug, and hardly any fight, he went off with the cops, who hauled him down to the 126th Street police station, where they stuck him in the juvenile pen, before taking him downtown to Centre Street for booking at night court, where he met his Legal Aid lawyer.

Because the shooting had taken place so close to Christmas and the victim was so pious, "a young man about to enter the seminary," reporters flocked to Claremont. Ives' telephone rang constantly. A photographer broke the faulty door lock in the entranceway and went upstairs to get a picture of whoever answered the door. Camping outside, television crews and newspaper reporters competed for tidbits of information. The kids and neighbors who knew the family said little to the press, aside from generalities, in an effort to respect a gentle father and the memory of his son.

And when it was learned that Ives had been involved in the community on behalf of poor children, and in particular those of Spanish-speaking descent, they made him out to be a saint who had been betrayed by the very kind of young person he had tried to help. Despite his suffering and pain, reporters hounded the poor man as he made his way to church or to the funeral parlor or just to the store.

In the newspapers, he read that his son's murderer was named Daniel Gomez. His mother was on welfare. He had two previous arrests for petty theft. He was an eighth-grade dropout, his father in jail. He had seven brothers and sisters and an extended family (even he, a family!). Ives read that Gomez' thirty-four-year-old mother wept uncontrollably at hearing the accusations and denied that her good son could have committed so heinous a crime. He noticed the word "heinous" again and again. At the time of the incident Gomez had just been to a movie on Ninety-sixth Street with his girl-friend and had been in a bad mood because of an argument about money. She was thirteen. He had bought the gun outside Alexander's department store on 152nd Street and Third Avenue a few months before for twenty dollars and was known in the neighborhood for bragging about how he was going to use it to get rich. A school report listed his IQ as average; some concern had been expressed by a Jewish social worker, who said the kid had blamed his problems in school on his principal, who was Jewish, and that he was convinced that all Jews were running the schools badly on purpose. Some neighbors said that he was basically a good boy, but others said he had been prone to violence since childhood. He had once tied an "ashcan" to a pigeon's neck and lit its fuse, laughing when the bird had been blown to pieces. He too also went to church and had just recently spent a morning shoveling snow for his parish, for free.

At fourteen he would be tried as a juvenile and, if convicted, he would be out on the streets in four years, tops. And what did Mr. Ives think of that? a journalist asked him. Ives, on his way down the street and feeling hounded, shrugged and said, "Please leave me alone."

But they managed to get a quote from one of the local priests, and this was used as a headline in two of the papers: GOD HAS CALLED HIM TO HEAVEN.

The Visible Man

Walking down the street, Ives could not look into anyone's eyes very long without his inward pain bringing tears to his eyes. He found himself wearing sunglasses all the time, night and day, and oddly, despite the darkness of his spirit, he wore a large crucifix given him by Carmen Ramirez and let it hang on his chest, visible to all. He remembered sitting for hours inconsolably in his son's room the night after he had died. He'd sat there examining a Revell model of a man that his son had kept on a shelf, the outer plastic shell transparent, the organs inside visible. He remembered when his boy, then twelve and wondering if he might one day become a doctor, had asked him to buy that model kit for Christmas. And when that Christmas had passed, Ives would find his son lying on his stomach in the living room, with a biology textbook open before him, dipping a brush into one or another small jar of airplane-model paint, trying to capture accurately the colors of the organs. He saw the miniature liver, kidneys, stomach, intestines, and all the rest set into place, and thought about his son.

The heart had been cut, the femoral artery in his hip torn in two, the coroner had whispered.

He saw the skeleton, the gallbladder with its deep purple coloration and the heart and all the veins shooting upward like tree roots throughout the body; for a few moments he imagined Jesus Christ himself on the Cross, Jesus trembling, as his son must have trembled in his last moments....

Glorious life ending. There must have been a moment when his son had gasped for air, the last time, as Jesus must have. But as Jesus had risen, he wanted his son to rise up, organs and spirit and mind intact, and everything to be as it had been not so long ago.

He sat there in his son's room thinking about the time when he had experienced the presence of God, *or of something,* on Madison Avenue, and for the life of him, he tried to imagine death as something transcendent and beautiful, as he had been taught to believe and had wanted to believe in those moments.

And now, he thought, his boy was dead, and even if he were to rise, to be reincarnated in some other form, their lives would not be the same. What was that little quotation from the New Testament that had once impressed him when he was a boy? A quotation he'd at one time always taken to heart, from I John 2:17: "... The world passeth away, and the lust thereof; but he that doeth the will of God abideth for ever." Was that so? Or was it that the world, their life, the familiar, the comfortable would not ever occur again?

Suddenly he began to feel a sorrowful nostalgia for the kind of afterlife that he had been raised to believe in, when he used to envision a pastoral setting in the clouds. People wore white robes and walked on a road that led to an eternal city where they could live in harmony with God and the good saints, in a state of perpetual love and comfort.... He thought of a book he had purchased a few years back, in his "searching" days after his "vision": something called *Human Personality and Its Survival of Bodily Death* by F. W. H. Myers, in which its author argued that all human beings, good and bad alike, had souls that existed into perpetuity, in an afterlife that he called an "eventuality," a kind of painless darkness. Memories and personalities would pass intact into eternity. And yet there was a flaw in that theory, as Ives saw it. There would be no God, no further development of the spirit, no change of being, just eternal recollections of what had once been, as if all memory and thoughts attained during a life were sent up invisibly into the night air, to exist in a godless, lightless afterlife, the image of which struck Ives as a kind of eternal death. Then he thought about his vision of the four swirling winds and interpreted them as an expression of supernatural folly and grew further depressed.

At a quarter to two in the morning, he allowed his face to slowly lower into the chalice of his hands, and he wept until he could not see.

Things Were in the Air

The wake lasted only a day and was held at an Amsterdam Avenue parlor, Kennedy's, not far from the church. Everyone from the neighborhood was there. The MacGuires came in from Long Island, Annie's three policeman brothers in their dress blues, with their shoulder cords and medals, sat in the back. Her father and mother and various cousins came and went throughout the day, but her brothers stayed, and going outside to smoke cigarettes, marched up and down the street in front of the parlor, Ives by their side, regarding all passersby, street drunks and junkies as well as decent citizens minding their own business, with contempt. A lot of strangers came with flowers, and so many prayer cards, rosaries, and crucifixes were left in Robert's coffin that every few hours a lady who worked for the parlor would come up to remove them. Young seminarians and many priests came by. A lot of neighborhood fellows came in around two in the afternoon, half drunk, paid their respects, and stood about the parlor entrance in thin-soled shoes shivering. Flowers arrived from New Jersey, where his friend Mr. Messmer lived. And he got a telephone call from Mr. Mannis in London; he had called during intermission of the theater where they were presenting *Stop the World I Want to Get Off,* with Anthony Newley. A number of Annie's teaching colleagues showed up or sent flowers, and about twenty-five people from the agency came, among them Mr. Freeman, who traveled on that soggy day with his wife and one of his sons from Chappaqua; Morty Silverman, Alvarez, Martinez, Dinnerstein, and Fuentes from the Spanish division of the company; many people from accounting; and secretaries from the sales department, some of whom came in from the Bronx and Queens.

Ives wore a blue suit and stood by the door, speaking with one of the parish priests and greeting, ever so quietly, people as they came in. But now and then he would look off toward the casket and turn his back on the people, as the darkest thoughts overwhelmed him, and he would have to compose himself again. Every so often Ramirez went up to him, took him by the arm, and whispered, "You are all right, my friend."

Annie and Caroline were in black. She was taking her brother's death badly. She spent much of that day sitting with her mother, holding her hand. Just a few days before he was shot one of Caroline's girlfriends had teased her about how she thought Robert kind of looked like one of the Beatles, Paul McCartney: "Too cute to be a priest." And now? There he lay, against a backdrop of flowers, a black rosary wrapped in his curled hands, and dozens of Mass cards for prayers to be said for his departed soul stuck in the silken creases by his side. Every so often, Ramirez' son, Pablo, came by to sit with her. He brought her a candy bar and he kept saying, "If you're hungry, let me know, okay?" At one point they took a walk over to Riverside Park, so that she could stretch her legs and get some air. They stood in the chill wind in a field of stark trees under a sullen sky, watching barges float by on the water, and because she was cold, he wrapped his arms around her and they kissed and held each other for a long time.

Ives' sister, Katherine, came to stay in the apartment and cooked their meals; Harry had flown in from San Diego with his third young pretty wife, and he dealt with the situation by giving Ives a check for a thousand dollars to help defray the costs, and said things like "Why you brought the kid up around here, in these times, is beyond me," again and again, a sentiment that Annie's family shared. In their opinion it seemed incomprehensible that decent people would even want to subject themselves to the noise and filth of the city, let alone expose themselves to the potential for violence.

Ives listened, and while a part of him thought these notions small-minded, another part of him blamed himself for not having brought his children up outside the city, as in Larchmont in Westchester, when he could have afforded it. In those moments, his liberal ideals were disturbed, and he found himself distressed that they had not moved years before. There had been that autumn day when he and Annie and the kids had taken a drive upstate and, getting lost, had found an old house that had been built in the 1920s, in the style called "Stockbroker Tudor," the kind that one saw in ads about happy families with wag-tailed dogs and gardens in the springtime and warm, homey parlors, bountiful tables, and stone fireplaces at Christmas, the kind of place that Ives had illustrated dozens of times—images from "another America" that he had somehow disregarded when it had come to his own family. It was situated on a beautiful piece of sloping land, near a decent small town and a train station, and, at the time, the property was being offered for a very good price. But Ives had decided against it because he did not want to leave the vitality of the neighborhood, or expose his children to the kind of well-intended but nevertheless narrow thinking of small towns, and because he had come to love the Puerto Ricans and Dominicans and Cubans who lived near them. But now his boy was dead.

During this time Ramirez and his wife had been invaluable and among the most respectful and sorrowful mourners. Juanito the barber came by with his family, as did Freddie Alvarez, owner of Freddie's Bodega, as had dozens of Spanish-speaking people from the neighborhood, like a certain lady of great dignity named Mireya, a nurse, who like many others said to Ives and Annie, "I'm really sorry that the boy who did it was Puerto Rican." And Ives would nod and then hear the same thing repeated, even while some of the Irish citizens of the neighborhood stood about by the doorway, figuring out ways to exact justice and revenge.

They buried his son on Christmas Eve morning, 1967, out in Long Island, his marker a simple Celtic cross. The burial was covered by the press, despite efforts to maintain privacy. A lot of important people came, few whom Ives knew. Zoom-lensed cameras captured the scene, and in an unfortunate gaffe, they published a picture of Celeste, Robert's former girlfriend, who had fallen apart and kept her distance from the family until the funeral, being held in Ives' arms, and identified her as his daughter....

Later, because it was Christmas, Ives had somehow felt compelled to leave the nice watch he'd bought his son in the room, instead of returning it to the store. He put it in his top drawer, as if his boy would come in anytime now to claim it. That drawer was stuffed with school paraphernalia, prayer cards, baseball cards, playing cards, a *Felix the Cat* comic that Ives had illustrated himself, years before. And pamphlets, a dozen of them, from different seminaries, clipped together, one of them with the sun's rays extending outward in the shape of a cross, the title: *In God's Service.* On a shelf Robert had an edition of the *World Book Encyclopedia,* which he had bought when he was ten with his own money; an *Oxford Book of Saints,* his marker left on the page describing Saint Francis of Assisi. A row of books on sciences, a picture book of pretty flowers from Celeste. A paperback novel called *Invasion of the Star Creatures* and a book on ancient Egypt. He saw that in a row on the inside cover his son had drawn three symbols: that of an ankh ☥, chrismon ☧, and crucifix ✝, one leading to the next. In a bag he found a copy of *Fanny Hill,* which had one of his son's friend's names in the margin, certain pages marked off. It made him laugh. Then on Robert's desk, where each night he had worked by lamplight on his schoolwork—what "good" youngsters do— he found an edition of *A Christmas Carol,* which Annie had given him, opened to one of the middle chapters.

He went to church and prayed for guidance, begging God to bring forgiveness into his heart. He would kneel before the crèche, the crucifix, and wonder how and why all these things had happened. At night he would dream of black threads twisting in the air and slipping into his body from afar. Though he bowed his head and trembled at the funeral, though he spoke kindly with the priests and repeated to himself a thousand times that God was good and that the manifestations of evil that come to men are ultimately explicable in some divine way, His wisdom greater than what any of them would ever know, Ives felt a great numbness descending over him.

What did it feel like? He felt the way that young girl whom he and Annie had once seen falling through the air had felt. Expression tormented, he spent a long time before the mirror, reading into his own face great foolishness. He did not like to look back and recall the last days of that *other* Ives. He wanted to be drunk. He had nothing to say. Getting two weeks' sympathy leave from the agency, he spent much of that time pacing up and down the hall and standing by the windows. It meant despairing about the supernatural and yet waiting every night for a supernatural event.

Ives and Annie slept, entangled in each other's arms, their daughter sleeping alone. Ives would get up a half-dozen times a night to make sure that she was resting. And every so often he would push the door open, intending to turn the radio off, but would find himself standing silently over her, his heart breaking whenever he would think about how much Robert's death must have pained her. And he would sometimes move closer, and, brushing aside the hair that fell over her brow, plant a tender kiss on her forehead. He would hear her sigh…. You know what it was like? It was like drowning.

There Was a Photograph

There was another photograph that ran in the newspapers, taken a few weeks after the funeral, when Ives met the Gomez family for the first time. This "meeting" was arranged by a priest, a Father Jimenez, a nearly Chinese-looking Puerto Rican man of about thirty, who turned up at Ives' door, black hat and New Testament in hand. "Perhaps the pain would be diminished if you met these people," the priest told him. "There's a lot of poison in the air: it would say something for you to go there."

And although Annie would have nothing to do with the boy's family, Ives, in the spirit of reconciliation, agreed to think about it.

A week passed and Ives, out of a notion of decency, and after going back and forth about it, called the priest.

"I'll go and see them," Ives said.

The Gomez family lived on 137th Street, in a tenement down the steep hill from City College. Ives had agreed under the condition that no one know, but when they turned up at around three one Sunday afternoon, there were photographers parked in a car across the street. The boy's grandmother, holding a rosary and with a mouthful of prayers, had been waiting on the stoop for them, and at the sight of Ives, with tears in her eyes, she begged for his forgiveness. Ives nodded and embraced her before going in.

As they walked up a stairway, they passed a window that opened onto a backyard filled with the residue of a recent snow, lumps of garbage, the hard edges of discarded boxes and bottles peeking out here and there. Then the apartment on the third floor: loud television from the living room, promptly turned off when the grandmother opened the door and shouted: "Angie, they're here. *Turn off the television!*"

A humble apartment, Ives thought, a poor family as the newspapers had said. And apparently very religious: he counted three crucifixes, one in the kitchen, one in the hall, one in the living room. Led inside, he was introduced to the boy's mother, Angie Gomez. She was an attractive woman with a bouffant hairdo, long earrings, heavy rouge on the cheeks and lipstick. High heels and tight slacks, a long rayon blouse and bracelets, as if she were getting ready for a party. Three of her other sons were in the room, and it seemed to Ives, as the introductions were made by the priest, that none of them wanted anything to do with what had happened. He had the impression that he had interrupted them as they watched a favorite movie on television. When Ives shook Mrs. Gomez' hand, she could barely manage to smile, and when her mother chided her about warming up a little bit for the *hombre simpático,* she suddenly exploded in one-hundred-words-a-minute Spanish, unaware that Ives could understand: "Don't tell me I'm being cold. You know that I didn't want to be here, but I'm doing this for you, mamá, but I don't think my son did shit, and if he did do something, I bet you he was provoked because he's not so stupid to do something like that out of the blue; and who is this man, anyway?"—these lines broken by an intermittent, nearly gracious smile. Ives sitting way out on the edge of the couch, with his hat in his hand, looked at the priest, wanting to go, and at the same time, wanting to make a point that his intentions were good.

"It's a sad thing that's happened," Ives softly said. "For all of us."

"Yes, we're so sorry about this," the grandmother said. And she started up about how they had tried to raise him in a correct manner, but with times being what they were, and with his father "away," there was only so much they could do. Ives nodded in sympathy.

Then the priest asked them to pray with him, to ask God to fill their hearts with forgiveness and understanding. But while they prayed Ives could not keep from looking at the woman, his eyes boring into her, because in this woman's scornful expression he read the story of her son's life: he had seen women like her many times on the street, young mothers who had gotten pregnant as teenagers, and hating it, dragged their kids along, slapping their faces, and saying, if the kids complained or gave them any kind of "lip" or cried, "You keep on, and I'll kick your ass, junior."

And it was as if she could read his mind. Suddenly, as if she herself had been accused of something, she broke off from the prayers and announced: "Look, everybody, I gotta go." And to Ives she said: "Mister, you really seem like a nice man, but I've got to tell you something. I feel really bad about what's happened to your son, but the fact is nobody knows who really did the shooting. You know how many kids walk around here with pistols? I feel really bad, but we don't owe you nothing, and we don't need this ... this show, okay? I've already got two boys who've gone to jail and now they want to put this one away too, and you come here without nobody proving a goddamn thing. You know why he's in trouble? Because of this." And she slapped at her own skin. "Because he's dark and Puerto Rican. I know he didn't do it, and that will come out. The cops picked him up because they had pressure to pick someone up. You know it, Father here knows it, everybody does. But I don't believe any of it and can tell you that just the fact that you're here makes us look bad. It's a dishonor, so forgive me if I can't apologize for something that my son didn't do."

Then to her mother in Spanish, *"No me mires así,"* or "Don't give me that look." And she lit a cigarette, and threw on a coat, and left the living room. Her mother, a tenor of shame to her words, said, "Ai, these young kids today." And, "I mean it sincerely, Señor Ives, that I will pray for your son's soul every day. I am—we are—so sorry."

There was little else that he could do except to leave.

Taken earlier when Ives and the priest had first arrived, the photograph showed the grandmother wrapping her arms around Mr. Ives, their expressions sorrowful, intensely sympathetic, perhaps even understanding. The headline above the photograph: "Forgiveness?"

The Dream

The kid had been released on bond, as he awaited trial, and that bit of information continued to distress Ives even after he had met with his family. He was not a drinker, but after work Ives would stop by the Biltmore to see Ramirez and have a few double scotches and then, on his way home, stop at Malloy's and have a few more and remain until he could hardly keep his eyes open. Such was his pain, at his lowest point, that he would tend to dally longer with each passing evening. Spending those nights in the bar, by the pool table, or lingering before the bathroom mirror, or watching the young men playing the pinball machine, he would find himself in that bar at midnight, conversations dimmed and then growing louder, images blurred before him.

Early one morning, with his eyes half closed, he listened as the men, with their own kids to worry about, speculated about what they could do to punish his son's murderer. He was so exhausted that it all struck him, or would be remembered, as a bad dream.

"What do you think, Ives, should we or shouldn't we?"

"Should you what?"

"Pop him."

"What?"

"Mr. Ives, like we've just finished telling you, and it doesn't have to go beyond my door. If you want us to hire someone to kill the son of a bitch who killed your kid, we'll do it."

Addressing Ives was Mr. Malloy, the owner. He was a burly, affable enough man, known as a small-time gangster, whom Ives would see in church on Sundays with his devout wife—Ives never saw her in the bar. Mr. Malloy then leaned closer and said gently, "Let me explain…" And he told Ives about how they had started collecting money for the purpose of hiring someone to "take care of business." Then he reached behind the bar and brought up a tin shortbread box which was filled with crumpled five- and ten-dollar bills. Ives held the box for a moment.

"Listen, Eddie," Malloy continued. "We got nothing against the Spanish. Guys like Ramirez are okay with us, but we don't want any of these people to think that they can fucking come over here and get away with murder. You know that if you go uptown into a Cuban or Puerto Rican neighborhood and try to pop someone, they'll kill you like that…."

"The Cubans?" Ives asked.

"And the mafia's like that too," another voice added.

"So the question is, what do we do? Do we take care of business? Or do we forget about it until this kid pops someone else? Come on, Ives, can we do it?"

Ives looked around him and found himself in the center of a circle of snarling wolves' faces.

"Please, I beseech you …"

"Beseech?" someone said indignantly. "Are we in the f—ing Bible?"

"Please," Ives was saying. "In good conscience I can't condone it. No."

But a part of him really wanted to say "Yes."

"Look, it wouldn't cost much to do it. We could even hire another spic to do it." Then (with sensitivity, for his closeness to the community was well known), "Sorry."

The word was that for a thousand dollars they could have a professional from Brooklyn shoot Gomez, but times were such that they could hire a kid for three hundred dollars off the street, and if they looked around, they could probably find someone who cost two hundred, maybe even one-fifty….

"Think about it, Eddie. The kid's walking free while your son is in the ground. Just say the word and his ass is grass."

Ives got home around two o'clock, didn't know how he got there, and woke up with his trousers and shoes still on. That day he had vague recollections of further arguments, voices coming back to him.

"What if he gets off and kills someone else?"

"... And just remember he'll be free anyway when he's eighteen. You think he'll have straightened out by then? How many kids you know who do time come back like priests?"

"What about justice for your son?"

"It won't bring him back, but at least we'll save the taxpayers money. And believe me you'll feel better, we all will."

"... Just remember, if you don't take care of business, no one else will. Do you really think God gives a shit?"

At work he thought about it. Had someone really made the offer, or had he been drunk or dreaming and imagined it?

Incidentally

The "bench" trial took place in the early spring of 1968 and attracted further publicity. The whole proceeding took about an hour, and the young man was convicted of second-degree manslaughter and sent up to the Spofford Detention Center in the Bronx, where he would remain until he turned eighteen. That morning Ives and Annie showed up in court, and their photographs were splashed all over the newspapers again. Sitting erect, a white purse on her lap, and not once turning her attention from the front of the courtroom, Annie gave an impression of stoicism and strength. As for Ives? Eyes red, his face gaunt, he seemed on the verge of weeping, and looked out at the courtroom with the weary expression of a man who had not slept well for months. He tried to sit still, but kept fidgeting. He wore a wool suit and regretted it, because the fabric was driving him nuts. He kept scratching himself. As he sat there, his knees ached from his many visits to church, where he had tried to understand the reasons why He had allowed his son's death. He had knelt so much that a terrible rash had erupted upon his kneecaps.

But that's not what Ives would mainly remember. There was a moment when the young man was being led away by a correction's officer, and he passed not three feet from where Ives and Annie were sitting. He was wearing a blue suit, white shirt, and blue tie. His thick and wavy black hair had been cut short, and despite the violence of his crime, and the setting, he could very well have been a young usher at a wedding. Ives was struck by his lack of expression, and by how young he seemed. He was a boy. And because of that, perhaps, Ives stood up and wanted him to look into his eyes, to see the pain that had become well known to others in the neighborhood. But the kid averted his eyes, and it so upset Ives that he tried to grab hold of the boy's arm as he was being led out by a guard, but could not reach him.

The kid would serve out a term of three years and seven months, and Ives' hair would turn white in the interim.

Guides to Reflection

1. Annie Ives tells the high school English class she teaches that the novelist Charles Dickens "believed that only a heartless society would leave its unfortunate poor to its sad fortune" *(Reader, 82)*. One of her students clearly believes that America is such a society. Review passages in the story that seem to support the student's judgment.

2. Throughout the story, Hijuelos is forthright about race relations in New York. Tensions between various racial groups are exacerbated by Robert's murder, and Ives' liberal ideals are tested. Discuss Hijuelos's handling of these racial tensions in the story.

3. After Robert's death, Ives is torn between his desire for revenge and his desire for forgiveness. Consider how he vacillates between these two things in the story. What difference does his faith make?

4. In the story, Hijuelos includes many details of the daily lives of each of the Iveses. He describes, for instance, both the appearance and demeanor of guests at the Iveses' Christmas party. He lists the records Robert purchased the day he died and the books on Robert's desk at home. He tells readers where Annie and Edward shopped and walked and what they ate. He details Caroline's unsettling experience at the apartment of the rich boy. Why does Hijuelos include so many specific details of everyday life in this story about Robert's death?

5

Reynolds Price

No one writing fiction today is more profoundly involved with the Bible than Reynolds Price. Raised in the Christ-haunted South, though not in an especially church-going family, he was fascinated early on in his life both by the narratives of the Old Testament (brought to vivid "DeMilleian" life in Hurlbut's *Story of the Bible*) and by the face of Jesus (searched for in a "packed anthology of guesses" served up by a book called *Christ and the Fine Arts).*[1] Price's interest in the Bible and the person of Christ are not especially obvious in his novels and stories, although they deal with themes of guilt and forgiveness, free will and determination, particularly as played out over the generations within a given family.

Nevertheless, when Price was looking for new direction at a pivotal point in his career he turned almost instinctively to the earliest stories he had ever encountered in print. He began doing "literal translations of short, almost blindingly lucid Bible stories," 50 of which were later gathered in *A Palpable God* (1978).[2] Almost two decades later his boyhood quest for the face of Jesus led him to translate the Gospels of Mark and John, and to append to them his own apocryphal life of Christ. These efforts at translation not only made him an apprentice of the master narrators of his family and region, but also put him in touch with the particular "news" he very much needed to hear: "news that our lives proceed in order toward a pattern which, if tragic here and now, is ultimately pleasing in the mind of a god who sees a totality and at last enacts His will."[3]

Price's personal life has not been without the experience of tragedy or lacked occasions to doubt the mind of God. In 1984, he suffered a bout with cancer that ultimately left him a paraplegic, confined to a wheel chair and dependent on the help of an assistant. He has written movingly of this experience in *A Whole New Life* (1994), not only about the devastation of illness but of what he has discovered as a result of his suffering: an increased sense of attentiveness to the world around him and a new freedom to write. Indeed, since the mid-1980s, Price has published more than 15 books, including novels and short stories as well as plays, essays, memoirs, and poetry. His most recent work, *Letter to a Man in the Fire* (1999), is a response to a young medical student stricken with cancer who also entertains questions as old as the book of Job: does God exist and does God care?

Price typically sets his fiction in the northeast counties of North Carolina, the region of his rural and small-town childhood, as well as of Duke University where he has taught English literature and creative writing since 1958. Describing why he situates his stories in this area Price says, "It's the place about which I have perfect pitch."[4] Although primarily a realistic writer, his work is shot through with a sense of the numinous and uncanny. Mystery lies just beneath the surface of the everyday world, glimpsed in fleeting moments of dream or vision, in visitations by ghosts or angels, and through the experience of mishap as well as exultation. His goal as a writer has been to make such moments palpable, to use his writer's "gift of tongues" to convey "a wordless knowledge of the core of light."[5]

Two brief trips to Israel in the early 1980s took Price out of his North Carolina milieu to a Holy Land where he found himself in quite direct contact not only with the landscape of the Bible, but inexplicably with the sacred itself. This profound encounter has left its mark on two stories in which a Christmas visit to a holy place leads a skeptical American traveler to discover depths he never wanted to plumb. In "An Early Christmas," positioned by Price at the very end of his *Collected Stories* (1993), the site of reckoning is the Church of the Holy Sepulchre. In "Long Night," set in Bethlehem rather than Jerusalem, it is the Church of the Nativity with its "trunk-sized niche where the manger stood" *(Reader, 106)*. Price has said of his own visit to Bethlehem, "[It's] not like Williamsburg. You can also see how it's no accident that people have been in a semi-insane contention for the rights to this place forever, for as long as we can remember in human history. There is something truly sacred about the place that makes you see how it can drive people almost crazy."[6]

In "Long Night" an American architect ends a trip to Israel with a visit to Bethlehem. His goal is the Chinese box construction of the ancient church, with its warren of holy places nested within a single unimposing structure. Drawn downward to the sacred cave where Jesus was born, compelled by "the nagging tendency to awe" he officially left behind in junior high, he finds himself moving inward. He thinks of his childhood world and revisits the sphere of the sacred in his own life. Suddenly, a mute Arab named Kamil interrupts his solitude and, in an effort to give the American a gift, literally opens a door on yet another depth, into a deeper darkness. A struck match reveals to the eye only "the family junkroom of Jesus' birthplace," but what the American visitor touches blindly with his hand is something—repeatedly referred to as "it"—that puts him in touch with the unnamable mystery of the place. At a loss for words himself, he can only listen in wonder to what the mute Kamil manages painfully to say in grunt after grunt: *real*. Everything in him wants to run away, but the Arab will not let go of his wrist. He must hear repeatedly the one word his companion can speak, the only one that matters—*real*.

Peter S. Hawkins

Notes

1. *Reynolds Price, Clear Pictures: First Loves, First Guides* (New York: Atheneum, 1989), 243. In chapter seven of this memoir, entitled "Credible Light," Price gives an account of his religious formation and experience. He offers a succinct statement of his mature faith in "At the Heart," found in *A Common Room: Essays 1954-1987* (New York: Atheneum, 1987), 402-405. For an appreciation of his identity as an "outlaw Christian," see Susan Ketchin's interview with him in her book, *The Christ-Haunted Landscape: Faith and Doubt in Southern Fiction* (Jackson, Miss.: University Press of Mississippi, 1994), 69-99.

2. Reynolds Price, "A Single Meaning: notes on the origins and life of narrative," in *A Common Room*, 248.

3. Ibid., 249.

4. Cited in Michael Ruhlman, "A Writer at His Best," *New York Times Magazine* (Sept. 20, 1987): 133.

5. "Credible Light," *Clear Pictures*, 262-263.

6. Interview with Susan Ketchin in *Christ-Haunted Landscape*, 98. See also Price's description of the Bethlehem church at Christmas in "An Early Christmas," *Collected Stories* (New York: Atheneum, 1993), 621-622. His protagonist reflects: "It was no disappointment; for all its gold and garish trim, the birth cave gives off that same primal force as caves where mankind sheltered ages past and left the shadows of their small hands and the beasts they worshiped, hunted and ate. Around the silver star in the floor that marks the birth-site (a star whose theft caused the Crimean war), I smelled the high iron odor of blood as if a girl had labored there not long ago; and I touched my brow to the points of the star as an Arab child had done just before me."

Long Night

In your rented Fiat, the size of a roller skate, you can drive south from the heart of Jerusalem and be in Bethlehem in fifteen minutes. It also makes an attractive walk—two gentle hours, no real climbing and the compact town strung out on its ridge as your visible goal through the clear desert day. That winter month, a dry December, I drove south a dozen times alone. Because I'm a licensed architect who veered into writing years ago, I was there to plan a commissioned piece on the Church of the Nativity, the town's great magnet. That big dim good-smelling warren of a place is the oldest continuously used church in Christendom and has a good deal to be said for it still as a showcase of Middle Eastern architecture from Constantine onward—a depressing good deal. The lines and pillars of the oldest church shame the Catholic and Greek Orthodox additions, a boatload of jimcrack pictures and lanterns—the eunuch Babe and his boneless Mother in cancer-causing pastel inks.

The beating heart of all that weight is a limestone cave. You walk toward the altar, then start down one of a pair of steep stairs. Twelve feet later, you're inside the cave. You look overhead, or steal a glance behind leather wall-hangings, to see the live stone. It's very much there despite two millennia of chiseling pilgrims. And trustworthy records that date to less than a century after Jesus' death say that here he was born, that simple a fact—a low space not as long as a schoolbus, which served as dry shelter for livestock and overflow guests from the nearby inn.

There's a silver star in a low corner niche that says "Here Jesus Christ was born of Virgin Mary." It was stolen early in the nineteenth century and caused the whole Crimean War before its return. Five yards away down three more steps is a trunk-sized niche where the manger stood, the feeding trough that served as a cradle on the night in question. When the emperor Constantine's mother came here in 339, she allegedly confiscated what was left and took it to Rome where it's still on view in St. Mary Major just under the altar, a few warped boards in a busy crystal-and-gold container.

Anyhow I was leaving for home the next day and had spent the morning in east Jerusalem, buying belated Christmas presents and a sidewalk lunch that either would or would not kill me. Then I napped for an hour on my narrow bed in the YMCA, an honorable hostel facing the famed King David Hotel with its high-rolling weird component of guests—American Jews and German civilians. I dreamed about a guided tour, where Jews walked Germans through Hebrew history, a long stage-pageant with actual blood. Though an Anglo-Saxon, since early boyhood in the 1930s I've dreamed I was Jewish and the prey of a hunting party of Germans who are blind but equipped with exquisite noses.

By the time I got my eyes full-open, the afternoon was more than half gone; and the sky had thinned to the good light-blue of your favorite workshirt, a billion years old. Most of the weary cells of my mind longed to fall back and sleep again. But a sensible lobe, the size of a nickel, said "Haul yourself down there one last time."

As I crested the rise to Manger Square, Kamil, the parking manager, hailed me; and I suddenly thought I knew why I'd come. Lying on the occupied West Bank, Bethlehem has dapper Arab police in dark blue and white, plus anxious young Israeli soldiers with Uzis primed. They sometimes deign to help with traffic in the packed town-center. But Kamil is strictly a free-will agent, a hometown boy who shepherds tourists to the scarce parking places with a hand ballet as good as any cop's in rush-hour Rome. He assisted me three or four times before I understood his problem. The boy is dumb—mute, unable to speak. He'll sound an occasional baritone note as he opens your door or shuts you in and waves you off with the small banknote you offer in thanks but not a word. Still his listening face is mostly as pleasant as his general mood, and he always sports a baseball cap in fire-truck red.

He loped toward me now, beckoning wildly with a barn-wide grin as he caught my face. I quickly knew I'd give him all my leftover shekels and not bother splurging at the airport tomorrow on the useless gewgaws of duty-free shops. I had about fifty dollars left; and Kamil had been my favorite Arab of the several dozen on this first visit who'd shown me the hawkeyed boundless kindness of their faith and tribe. And since he seemed to go home at dark, I'd give it to him now.

As I braked to park, he was at my window with the eager smile of a child actor; but I took a moment to see who was near us. A bus was loading German nuns a few yards away, all stout and grim. Their hard eyes blocked my immediate plan but I hatched another. I got out, locked up and shook young Kamil's eager hand. Then I risked a question, "Will you have coffee with me?"

The smile disappeared; he was painfully baffled. Had I somehow offended or was he deaf too? A local waiter had said he was mute; I forgot to ask about his hearing.

I pointed across the square to a restaurant, St. George's (he of dragon fame, other local-boy-made-good, after David and Jesus—a fair enough record for a town you could lose in a block of Manhattan).

Kamil shook his head.

"Coffee? *Caffé?*" In the air, I drank from a nonexistent cup.

He finally got it. The smile beamed on and he took off his fingerless right-hand glove to shake my hand again, skin to skin.

The air was still warm; the outdoor tables were all but empty. So we sat outside and faced each other like players in a game. Musa, the waiter who'd also befriended me, showed no surprise. He met us with benign self-possession and eyes that could drill through armor plate, and may get the chance, but showed no hint of disdain for Kamil. Yet a dumb and grubby unofficial parker must have stood ten rungs down on the ladder from a spotless waiter.

And though I had a moment of panic—what would I say or do for these minutes?—once coffee came, the time went smoothly.

Kamil pocketed his cap, hand-combed his tan hair; and when he'd had his first long sip, he lapsed at once into what seemed a trance of meditative calm. The harried cords and lines of worry melted inward. In under ten seconds, he showed for the first time his actual age, maybe thirty-five.

Much older than I'd guessed. So I took his lead and also lapsed and was well away in thoughtless peace when Kamil bolted to his feet and waved at a bus that was struggling to park. I wanted to stop him, but he had his job so I nodded "Go."

He gave a quick but sweeping salaam like a movie sheik. Then the grin resumed and he jogged toward the bus that obligingly needed serious guidance. As ever, once the motor died, Kamil took his place by the door and met each tourist, dead in the eyes. He never appeared to expect a tip, and I never saw him get one. It seemed enough to search their faces—maybe news from where he'd never go.

I lapsed off again and watched the dance of some evening birds high over the church. They had the curved-wing shape of swallows but were twice the size of swallows at home. They went on tumbling with the fixed intent of carnivorous raptors. So as a further aid to calm, I chose the smallest bird and watched her weave through all the rest. Her rapid patterns calmed me too well. For actual minutes I never thought once of the son I'd lost five months ago, not to mention my present aim in a town that was known for births. And when the flock dissolved in space and I came to Earth, it was nearly dusk. The church would shut at the last trace of light. The square was empty of all but children. Kamil was nowhere in sight, surely gone. Another American charity foiled.

The church was open but the inside was dark and looked utterly empty. I'd walked a good halfway up the nave before I thought I might get locked in. By then I was reckless and pushed ahead. Any healthy person could do a lot worse than spend a night on the cold cave-floor. And the farther I went, the darker things got till, up near the altar, I was feeling the air itself for directions. I'd never longed for a Greek monk before, that surly breed, but I almost did. And then the precipitous stairs were at me—slick stone, no railing—and I almost fell.

The cave though was lighted, the usual candles and hanging oil lamps secreting a moist enfolding heat. Still no other human in sight. There are no chairs or benches, so you have two choices of respectful posture, standing or kneeling. I have a trick knee and in any case am not given to kneeling. I also have a nagging tendency to awe at the ancient sites of any faith that doesn't advocate a slaughter of the faithless, but prayer and prostration are matters I retired from in junior-high.

Still, there alone for maybe ten minutes, I came as near a physical bow as I'd come for decades. The thing my mind kept going back to was, some brand of touch. I'd bend my good knee and press my forehead—forehead, not lips— on the famous star. I told myself I could do the same at a few other places, like Keats's tombstone or the sill of a hut at the back of my grandfather's vegetable garden where an old black man, born a slave, had died after tending my childhood with well-meant patience. And I did step forward and start to crouch before I heard footsteps on the stairs. This would be the mad monk with beard aflame.

Instead it was Kamil—unsmiling, bareheaded again, even older. He came straight toward me and took my right hand; his gloves were gone.

He had never followed me before. I was glad of course and pressed his palm.

But his head shook hard. Then his face came down; and with lips so dry they scraped my skin, he kissed the heel of my hand by the thumb.

I thought that was more than a fair return on one cup of coffee; and I laid my other hand on the crown of his bowed head, the kind of blessing you see in paintings of Abraham or Isaac and Jacob. I knew I would never do it elsewhere above ground in daylight, but here it felt apt.

When he stood back up, Kamil still hadn't smiled. He moaned a low note, no word but no grunt. And he turned to leave.

I may be a hack but I can be moved, every year or so. I called his name in two clear syllables, "Ka - mil."

He stopped in his tracks but didn't look round.

So I thought "He can hear." And I covered the ten feet of cave between us, pressed my gift in his hand and shut his fingers on it.

He looked down slowly, then carefully opened the dingy wad of shekels. On his fingers he counted meticulously. Then grinning wide, he folded them back and thrust the wad into my breast pocket.

I said "No. For you, my friend."

He kept on grinning but shook his head.

When I reached to my pocket and tried to insist, Kamil pointed to the star and raised a hushing finger to his lips. Many Arabs in Bethlehem are Maronite Christians, and Muslims honor Jesus as a prophet, so I understood him to mean "Pipe down." By then I had the money out again.

But his head shook hard; and when I said "Please" in a lower voice, his eyes went fierce and his dry right hand came up and covered my offensive mouth. Now he'd muted me, he still didn't smile. But a sudden idea lit in his eyes. The hand came down and he moved past me toward the end of the cave, waving me on like a smoking bus. By the time I joined him, he'd shouldered aside a leather curtain and pointed to a low door set in the rock.

It looked as old as the smoky stone. But closer by, I saw it was wood with an ancient iron latch and lock. Any instant a monk would howl down on us or burst through the door with a flashing blade.

Kamil paused to test the silence. We might as well have been on Neptune. Then he fished in his trousers and brought out a key, four inches long, as black as the door and older looking. It turned the lock, and the door crept open at its own slow rate on a blacker space than any I've seen in years of walking through nights in the mountains with no city lights for fifty miles.

But when Kamil took my elbow to guide me, I didn't resist and didn't feel strange. The cave itself was country as strange as the back of Tibet. In three short steps we were in the deep dark, and the door shut behind us. We stood there awhile.

Kamil kept a strong grip on my arm, but that and the wide-spaced sound of his breath was all that let me know he was with me. For a second I thought of movie theaters in childhood summers—how I'd enter from a sun-drenched street and be blind at the top of the aisle, groping my way and sometimes sitting on a lady's lap before I could see. But as long as we waited, maybe two minutes, my eyes never widened enough to find light.

Then Kamil, nudged me forward again and brought my left hand down onto something. Dry wood apparently, the edge of something that felt man-made, some two feet long. I didn't want to go past the edge to explore. My hand must have stiffened; and still pitch-dark in a voice that resembled his parking grunts, Kamil said something. Some way, this time, I thought it was a word. I said "Beg your pardon?"

He waited in place and again repeated what was surely a word, though I still failed to hear it. Then he turned my arm loose and fumbled in his clothes.

That was when I balked. What in God's name would come down next? I wouldn't stay to watch. I turned back toward what I thought was the door.

But a quick light flared. Kamil had struck a long kitchen-match and was holding it out. We were in a walled-off deeper niche of the same birth cave. It was ten feet long with raw stone walls and a random huddle of junk on the ground. I could make out oil lamps, a stack of icons and whatever thing I'd just now touched on a shelf at waist level. I walked back toward it.

It was coated with an even layer of dust except where Kamil and I had disturbed it. But at first I could only think of a boat. It looked like an antique child's canoe, roughly gouged from a straight tree-trunk and a good deal longer than my hand had guessed, maybe three feet long by two feet wide. Oddly I pictured the infant Moses afloat on the Nile in his bulrush boat.

The match burned down; Kamil lit a second.

In the moment of dark between them, I managed to guess this was some kind of manger, something the monks kept hid away for processions upstairs. I met Kamil's grin with a grateful nod—an average tourist seldom glimpses the family junkroom of Jesus' birthplace.

Again he took my hand and thrust it to the scooped-out bottom of the manger. I felt it and, this time, thought of my mother's old bread-kneading bowl, a fine smooth oak but sold at her death for under a dollar. I even paused to want it back. The second match was dead by then.

The voice that had made Kamil's dumb grunts now said a word.

I thought it was *real*. He had said the word *real,* and he somehow meant this wood trough here. We were back in absolute dark again; and the trough was still not glowing or pulsing, nothing my eyes could read as uncanny. But too much was coming at me too fast—this changing man and his awful place, the thick taste of dark and whatever wooden worn old thing my fingers touched. I only knew I must not ask Kamil to speak again. I must leave here now. I tried to slide my hand from his grip.

Strong as anyone I'd ever known, the man that held me rung my wrist with a huge warm hand and said again *"Real"*—the same one word, many times through the night.

Guides to Reflection

1. "Long Night" is quite a short story and yet it manages to cover a significant amount of territory in its few pages. Beginning in Jerusalem, it moves on to Bethlehem's Manger Square; next we enter the Church of the Nativity, step down into the shrine of the Cave and then, thanks to Kamil's arrival on the scene, pass through a "low door set in the rock" that opens onto what is either a "junkroom" or a shrine within a shrine. What is the effect of this zeroing in and moving ever downward?

2. We never learn the name of the American architect who is the protagonist of this story and know only a few things about him. What are these details, and why do the circumstances of this visit to Bethlehem evoke them?

3. Kamil is in many ways inscrutable to the American visitor: a foreigner, to begin with, and a man able to gesture but not to speak. Yet he becomes in effect the protagonist's mentor and guide—the Virgil to his Dante—and, almost miraculously, is given the story's most significant word. How would you describe the various roles he plays in "Long Night"?

4. Price italicizes the word *real*, as if it came from a language other than English, and in order to underscore its importance. What are its multiple meanings—to Kamil, to the protagonist, to you—especially as you consider the Church of the Nativity as the story's setting?

5. In the history of Christianity, the churches marking Christ's birth and death have offered pilgrims the most treasured holy ground. Yet we see in the story how these traditional sites and relics also put the protagonist in touch with his mundane past: a hut on his grandfather's property, the pitch black movie theaters of his childhood summers, and his mother's "old bread-kneading bowl." What are the connections between the Church of the Nativity and these recollections? What have been the holy places or objects in your own life?

6

Louise Erdrich

When an interviewer asked Louise Erdrich if she feels like an outsider, she replied, "Sure, always an outsider, but that's a gift for a writer.... People who belong don't become writers, they're immersed and have no edge."[1] Erdrich's "edge" has been honed by the various perspectives she brings to her craft as writer. Of Native American, French, and German ancestry, Erdrich was born in 1954 in Minnesota and grew up in Wahpeton, North Dakota, where her parents taught at the Bureau of Indian Affairs boarding school. Her grandfather, Patrick Gourneau, was for a time tribal chairman at the Turtle Mountain Chippewa Reservation in north central North Dakota. After graduating from high school, Erdrich moved East, earning a bachelor's degree from Dartmouth in Hanover, New Hampshire, and a master's degree from Johns Hopkins in Baltimore.

For several years Erdrich lived first in North Dakota and then in Boston. She held a series of jobs, including poet for the North Dakota State Arts Council, waitress, beet weeder, construction flag signaler, and editor, while she worked at establishing herself as a writer. In 1981 Erdrich became a writer-in-residence at Dartmouth, remaining in New Hampshire for a decade before moving first to Montana and then to Minneapolis.[2]

Since her first books, a collection of poetry entitled *Jacklight* and the novel *Love Medicine,* were published in 1984, Erdrich has written a second collection of poetry, seven novels, two books for children, and a memoir, *The Blue Jay's Dance* (1995), in which she reflects on the first years of her three daughters' lives. While all her work has drawn critical attention, it is her novels that have established Erdrich as an important writer. In *Love Medicine,* which won the National Book Critics Circle Award, Erdrich introduces a number of characters who reappear in several of her later novels: *Beet Queen* (1986), *Tracks* (1988), *The Bingo Palace* (1994), and *Tales of Burning Love* (1996). Set primarily in North Dakota, these stories explore the lives of Native American, mixed blood, and Euro-American characters from 1912 to the present. Erdrich's characters in these novels, as well as in her most recent novel, *The Antelope Wife* (1998), struggle with questions of identity, with economic catastrophes, epidemics, racial tension, the land policies of the United States government, and with love, work, family, and community issues.

In addition to her own novels, Erdrich coauthored two others, *Crown of Columbus* (1991) and *Route Two* (1991), with her late husband, Michael Dorris, a professor of anthropology and founder of the Native American Studies Program at Dartmouth. Like Erdrich, Dorris was a critically acclaimed author of novels and memoir. Erdrich and Dorris detailed in interviews how they collaborated, discussing ideas for all their novels and editing each other's manuscripts.[3] Theirs was a remarkable, fruitful, literary partnership that ended tragically with Dorris's suicide in April 1997. Dorris's best-known work is his book *The Broken Cord* (1989), the story of how fetal alcohol syndrome affected his elder son, one of three children he adopted before marrying Erdrich.

In the novels that bear her name alone, Erdrich uses distinctive techniques that give these works a luminous, multifaceted quality. Erdrich rarely tells stories in chronological order, but instead creates a kaleidoscopic effect by moving in each chapter to a different time period. Moreover, rather than using one narrator to tell the story as most novelists do, Erdrich uses multiple first-person narrators. This means the reader adopts different points of view as the characters tell, in separate chapters, their versions of the events the novel relates. The great variety of characters Erdrich creates makes this an especially intriguing technique. Some of her characters are savvy, some are wise, and some survive extraordinarily difficult circumstances, but some are crazed, some are confused, some are unpredictable, and some are in deep despair.

Religious themes and characters are common in Erdrich's novels. Most often, the varieties of religious belief Erdrich explores are Native American religion and Roman Catholicism. In *Tracks,* for instance, the characters Fleur and Nanapush maintain strong ties to a mystical, visionary, Native American religion grounded in nature. Erdrich's treatment of Native American religion is most often elegiac, while her more frequent presentation of Roman Catholicism is more varied and complex. The priest Father Damien appears in the novels as a friend, albeit an ineffectual one, to Native Americans who suffer because of epidemics and government policies. Sister Leopolda, a much more important character than Father Damien, strongly influences several major characters in the novels. Crazed and perverse, Leopolda practices self-mortification and abuses children, yet she is seen as saintly by the other sisters and by priests. Apparently softening as years pass, she appears as a ghost after her death to advise and save the life of a woman who has chosen to write a book about her. While supernatural presences and the remnants of Native American beliefs prove beneficent in some of Erdrich's writing, the more common presentation of religion is typified in the problematic Leopolda.

A powerful but problematic religious experience dominates "Satan: Hijacker of a Planet," a short story that appeared in *The Atlantic Monthly* in August 1997. In "Satan," a woman recalls her sixteen-year-old self meeting a strong and determined itinerant preacher, Stan Anderson. Stan's sermon captivates her with its images and effective cadences, but the healing Stan and his associates attempt after the worship service falters until the girl sits by the bedside and conjures visions of nature that provide relief to the sufferer. These powerful and potentially good aspects of the religious experience are tempered, though, by other elements. The girl's ability to conjure the "pictures" developed as a means to escape her parents' fights. The "pictures" provide her only temporary relief, which is all they seem to offer the ill as well. And Stan's sermon, while highly effective, rings with right-wing rhetoric from the fringes of American Protestantism. Stan warns his listeners against using credit cards, parses the biblical meaning of current geopolitical events, and analyzes numbers signifying evil. Stan's own name is only one letter removed from "Satan," a highly suggestive coincidence. Stan calls Lucifer (whose name means "light") the "hijacker of a planet" *(Reader, 119)* as a way of describing the deceptive and then overwhelming reality of evil. The girl tells us she was drawn to Stan the way a deer is drawn to a light hunters use to lure deer for an easy kill. Perhaps, Erdrich seems to suggest, Stan's religious beliefs and practices offer the girl an escape from her arid, tumultuous home, but might they themselves not be just another form of evil? In "Satan," Erdrich masterfully evokes the experience of a girl who happens on a commanding religious figure and then struggles to understand her reaction to him. This story raises, as so many of Erdrich's explorations of religious experience do, searing questions about the sources, the nature, and the effects of religious belief.

Paula J. Carlson

Notes

1. Nancy Feyl Chavkin and Allan Chavkin, editors, *Conversations with Louise Erdrich and Michael Dorris* (Jackson, Miss.: University Press of Mississippi, 1994), 250.

2. *Contemporary Authors: New Revision Series*, vol. 62, s.v. "Louise Erdrich."

3. Chavkin, 185-188, 245-246.

Satan: *Hijacker of a Planet*

On the outskirts of a small town in the West, on an afternoon when rain was promised, we sat upon the deck of our new subdivision ranchette and watched the sky pitch over Hungry Horse. It was a drought-dry summer, and in the suspension of rain everything seemed to flex. The trees stretched to their full length, each leaf open. I could almost feel the ground shake the timbers under my feet, as if the great searching taproots of the lodgepole pines all around trembled. Lust. Lust. Still, the rain held off. I left my mother sitting in her chair and went to the old field behind the house, up a hill. There the story seemed even likelier. The wind came off the eastern mountains, smelling like a lake, and the grass reached for it, butter-yellow, its life concentrated in its fiber mat, the stalks so dry they gave off puffs of smoke when snapped. Grasshoppers sprang from each step I took, tripped off my arms, legs, glasses. I saw a small pile of stones halfway up the hill, which someone had cleared once, when this was orchard land. I sat down and continued to watch the sky as, out of nowhere, great solid-looking clouds built hot stacks and cotton cones. The trend was upward, upward, until you couldn't feel it anymore. I was sixteen years old.

I was looking down the hill, waiting for the rain to start, when his white car pulled into our yard. The driver was a big man, built long and square just like the Oldsmobile. He was wearing a tie and a shirt that was not yet sweaty. I noticed this as I was walking back down the hill. I was starting to notice these things about men—the way their hips moved when they hauled feed or checked fence lines. The way their forearms looked so tanned and hard when they rolled up their white sleeves after church. I was looking at men not with intentions, because I didn't know yet what I would have done with one if I got him, but with a studious mind.

I was looking at them just to figure, for pure survival, the way a girl does. The way a farmer, which my dad was before he failed, gets to know the lay of the land. He loves his land, so he has to figure how to cultivate it—what it needs in each season, how much abuse it will sustain, what in the end it will yield.

And I, too, in order to increase my yield and use myself right, was taking my lessons. I never tried out my information, though, until the man arrived, pulled with a slow crackle into our lake-pebble driveway. He got out and looked at me where I stood in the shade of my mother's butterfly bush. I'm not saying that I flirted right off. I didn't know how to. I walked into the sunlight and looked him in the eye.

"What are you selling?" I smiled, and told him that my mother would probably buy it, since she had all sorts of things—a pruning saw you could use from the ground, a cherry pitter, a mechanical apple peeler that also removed the seeds and core, a sewing machine that remembered all the stitches it had sewed. He smiled back at me and walked with me to the steps of the house.

"You're a bright young lady," he said, though he was young himself. "Stand close. You'll see what I'm selling by looking into the middle of my eyes."

He pointed a finger between his eyebrows.

"I don't see a thing," I told him, as my mother came around the corner, off the deck out back, holding a glass of iced tea in her hand.

While they were talking, I didn't look at Stan Anderson. I felt challenged, as if I were supposed to make sense of what he did. At sixteen I didn't have perspective on the things men did. I'd never gotten a whiff of that odor that rolls off them like an acid. Later only a certain look was required, a tone of voice, a word, no more than a variation in the way he drew breath. A dog gets tuned that way, sensitized to an exquisite degree, but it wasn't like that in the beginning. I took orders from Stan as if I were doing him a favor—the way, since I'd hit my growth, I'd taken orders from my dad.

My dad, who was at the antiques store, gave orders only when he was tired. All other times he did the things he wanted done himself. My dad was not, in the end, the man I should have studied if I wanted to learn cold survival. He was too ineffective. All my life my parents had been splitting up. I lived in a no-man's-land between them, and the ground was pitted, scarred with ruts, useless. And yet no matter how hard they fought each other, they stuck together. He could not get away from my mother, somehow, nor she from him. So I couldn't look to my father for information on what a man was—nor could I look to my grandfather. Gramp was too nice a man. You should have seen him when he planted a tree.

"A ten-dollar hole for a two-bit seedling," he'd say. That was the way he dug, so as not to crowd the roots. He kept the little tree in water while he pried out any rocks that might be there, though our land was just as good as Creston soil, dirt that went ten feet down in that part of Montana, black as coal, rich as tar, fine as face powder. Gramp put the bare-root tree in and carefully, considerately even, sifted the soil around the roots, rubbing it to fine crumbs between his fingers. He packed the dirt in; he watered until the water pooled. Looking into my grandfather's eyes I would see the knowledge, tender and offhand, of the way roots took hold in the earth.

I saw no such knowledge in Stan's eyes. I watched him from behind my mother. I discovered what he had to sell.

"It's Bibles, isn't it?" I said.

"No fair." He put his hand across his heart and grinned at the two of us. He had seen my eyes flicker to the little gold cross in his lapel. "Something even better."

"What?" my mother asked.

"Spirit."

My mother turned and walked away. She had no time for conversion attempts. I was only intermittently religious, but I suppose I felt that I had to make up for her rudeness, and so I stayed a moment longer. I was wearing very short cutoff jeans and a little brown T-shirt, tight—old clothes for dirty work. I was supposed to help my mom clean out her hobby brooder house that afternoon, to set in new straw and wash down the galvanized feeders, to destroy the thick whorls of ground-spider cobwebs and shine the windows with vinegar and newspapers. All my stuff, rags and buckets, was scattered behind me on the steps. And, as I said, I was never all that religious.

"We'll be having a meeting tonight," he said. "I'm going to tell you where."

He always told in advance what he was going to say; that was the preaching habit in him. It made you wait and wonder in spite of yourself.

"Where?" I said finally.

As he told me the directions, how to get where the tent was pitched, as he spoke to me, looking full on with the whole intensity of his blue gaze, I was deciding that I would go, without anyone else in my family, to the fairground that evening. Just to study. Just to see.

I drove a small sledge and a tractor at the age of eleven, and a car back and forth into town, with my mother in the passenger seat, when I was fourteen. So I often went where I wanted to go. The storm had veered off. Disappointed, we watched rain drop across the valley. We got no more than a slash of moisture in the air, which dried before it fell. In town the streets were just on the edge of damp, but the air was still thin and dry. White moths fluttered in and out under the rolled flaps of the revival tent, but since the month of August was half spent, the mosquitoes were mainly gone. Too dry for them, too. Even though the tent was open-sided, the air within seemed close, compressed, and faintly salty with evaporated sweat. The space was three-quarters full of singing people, and I slipped into one of the rear rows. I sat on a gray metal folding chair, just sat there, keeping my eyes open and my mouth shut.

He was not the main speaker, I discovered, and I didn't see him until the one whom the others had come to hear finished a prayer. He called Stan to the front with a little preface. Stan was newly saved, endowed with a message from the Lord, and could play several musical instruments. We were to listen to what the Lord would reveal to us through Stan's lips. He took the stage. A white vest finished off his white suit, and a red-silk shirt with a pointed collar. He started talking. I can tell you what he said just about word for word, because after that night and long away into the next few years, sometimes four or five times in one day, I'd hear it over and over. You don't know preaching until you've heard Stan Anderson. You don't suffer with Christ, or fear loss of faith, a barbed wire ripped from your grasp, until you've heard it from Stan Anderson. You don't know subjection, the thorough happiness of letting go. You don't know how light and comforted you feel, how cherished.

I was too young to stand against it.

The stars are the eyes of God, and they have been watching us from the beginning of the world. Do you think there isn't an eye for each of us? Go on and count. Go on and look in The Book and add up all the nouns and adverbs, as if somehow you'd grasp the meaning of what you held if you did. You can't. The understanding is in you or it isn't. You can hide from the stars by daylight, but at night, under all of them, so many, you are pierced by the sight and by the vision.

Get under the bed!

Get under the sheet!

I say to you, Stand up, and if you fall, fall forward!

I'm going to go out blazing. I'm going to go out like a light. I'm going to burn in glory. I say to you, Stand up!

And so there's one among them. You have heard Luce, Light, Lucifer, the Fallen Angel. You have seen it with your own eyes, and you didn't know he came upon you. In the night, and in his own disguises, like the hijacker of a planet, he fell out of the air, he fell out of the dark leaves, he fell out of the fragrance of a woman's body, he fell out of you and entered you as though he'd reached through the earth.

Reached his hand up and pulled you down.

Fell into you with a jerk.

Like a hangman's noose.

Like nobody.

Like the slave of night.

Like you were coming home and all the lights were blazing and the ambulance sat out front in the driveway and you said, *Lord, which one?*

And the Lord said, *All of them.*

You, too, follow, follow, I'm pointing you down. In the sight of the stars and in the sight of the Son of Man. The grace is on me. Stand up, I say. *Stand.* Yes, and yes, I'm gonna scream, because I like it that way. Let yourself into the gate. Take it with you. In four years the earth will shake in its teeth.

Revelations. Face of the beast. In all fairness, in all fairness, let us quiet down and let us think.

Stan Anderson looked intently, quietly, evenly, at each person in the crowd and spoke to each one, proving things about the future that seemed complicated, like the way the Mideast had shaped up as such a trouble zone. How the Chinese armies were predicted in Tibet and that came true, and how they'll keep marching, moving, until they reach the Fertile Crescent. Stan Anderson told about the number. He slammed his forehead with his open hand and left a red mark. *There,* he yelled, gutshot, *there it will be scorched.* He was talking about the number of the beast, and said that they would take it from your Visa card, your Mastercard, your household insurance. That already, through these numbers, you are under the control of last things and you don't know it.

The Antichrist is among us.

He is the plastic in our wallets.

You want credit? Credit?

Then you'll burn for it, and you will starve. You'll eat sticks, you'll eat black bits of paper, your bills, and all the while you'll be screaming from the dark place, *Why the hell didn't I just pay cash?*

Because the number of the beast is a computerized number, and the computer is the bones, it is the guts, of the Antichrist, who is Lucifer, who is pure brain.

Pure brain got us to the moon, got us past the moon.

The voice of lonely humanity is in a space probe calling, *Anybody home? Anybody home out there?* The Antichrist will answer. The Antichrist is here, all around us in the tunnels and webs of radiance, in the microchips; the great mind of the Antichrist is fusing in a pattern, in a destiny, waking up nerve by nerve.

Serves us right. Don't it serve us right not to be saved?

It won't come easy. Not by waving a magic wand. You've got to close your eyes and hold out those little plastic cards.

Look at this!

He held a scissors high and turned it to every side so that the light gleamed off the blades.

The sword of Michael! Now I'm coming. I'm coming down the aisle. I'm coming with the sword that sets you free.

Stan Anderson started a hymn and walked down the rows of chairs, singing. Every person who held out a credit card he embraced, and then he plucked that card out of their fingers. He cut once, crosswise. Dedicated to the Lord! He cut again. He kept the song flowing, walked up and down the rows cutting, until the tough, trampled grass beneath the tent was littered with pieces of plastic. He came to me last of all, and noticed me, and smiled.

"You're too young to have established a line of credit," he said, "but I'm glad to see you here."

Then he stared at me, his eyes the blue of winter ice, cold in the warmth of his tanned blondness, so chilling I just melted.

"Stay," he said. "Stay afterward and join us in the trailer. We're going to pray over Ed's mother."

So I did stay. It didn't sound like a courting invitation, but that was the way I thought of it at the time, and I was right. Ed was the advertised preacher, and his mother was a sick, sick woman. She lay flat and still on a couch at the front of the house trailer, where she just fit end to end. The air around her was dim, close with the smell of sweat-out medicine and what the others had cooked and eaten—hamburger, burnt onions, coffee. The table was pushed to one side, and chairs were wedged around the couch. Ed's mother, poor old dying woman, was covered with a white sheet that her breathing hardly moved. Her face was caved in, sunken around the mouth and cheeks. She looked to me like a bird fallen out of its nest before it feathered, her shut eyelids bulging blue, wrinkled, beating with tiny nerves. Her head was covered with white wisps of hair. Her hands, just at her chest, curled like little pale claws. Her nose was a large and waxen bone.

I drew up a chair, the farthest to the back of the eight or so people who had gathered. One by one they opened their mouths, rolled their eyes or closed them tight, and let the words fly out until they began to garble and the sounds from their mouths resembled some ancient, dizzying speech. At first I was so uncomfortable with all the strangeness, and even a little faint from the airlessness and smells, that I breathed in with shallow gulps and shut the language out. Gradually, slowly, it worked its way in anyway, and I began to *feel* its effect—not hear, not understand, not listen.

The words are inside and outside of me, hanging in the air like small pottery triangles, broken and curved. But they are forming and crumbling so fast that I'm breathing dust, the sharp antibiotic bitterness, medicine, death, sweat. My eyes sting, and I'm starting to choke. All the blood goes out of my head and down along my arms into the ends of my fingers, and my hands feel swollen, twice as big as normal, like big puffed gloves. I get out of the chair and turn to leave, but he is there.

"Go on," he says. "Go on and touch her."

The others have their hands on Ed's mother. They are touching her with one hand and praying, the other palm held high, blind, feeling for the spirit like an antenna. Stan pushes me, not by making any contact, just by inching up behind me so I feel the forcefulness and move. Two people make room, and then I am standing over Ed's mother. She is absolutely motionless, as though she were a corpse, except that her pinched mouth has turned down at the edges so that she frowns into her own dark unconsciousness.

I put my hands out, still huge, prickling. I am curious to see what will happen when I do touch her—if she'll respond. But when I place my hands on her stomach, low and soft, she makes no motion at all. Nothing flows from me, no healing powers. Instead I am filled with the rushing dark of what she suffers. It fills me suddenly, as water from a faucet brims a jug, and spills over.

This is when it happens.

I'm not stupid; I have never been stupid. I have pictures. I can get a picture in my head at any moment, focus it so brilliant and detailed that it seems real. That's what I do, what I started when my mom and dad first went for each other. When I heard them downstairs, I always knew a moment would come. One of them would scream, tearing through the stillness. It would rise up, that howl, and fill the house, and then one would come running. One would come and get me and hold me. It would be my mother, smelling of smoked chicken, rice, and coffee grounds. It would be my father, sweat-soured, scorched with cigarette smoke from the garage, bitter with the dust of his fields. Then I would be somewhere in no-man's-land, between them, and that was the unsafest place in the world. So I would leave it. I would go limp and enter my pictures.

I have a picture. I go into it right off when I touch Ed's mother, veering off her thin pain. Here's a grainy mountain, a range of deep-blue Missions hovering off the valley in the west. Their foothills are blue, strips of dark-blue flannel, and their tops are cloudy walls. The sun strikes through once, twice, a pink radiance that dazzles patterns into their faces so that they gleam back, moon-pocked. Watch them, watch close, Ed's mother, and they start to walk. I keep talking until I know she is watching too. She is dimming her lights, she is turning as thin as tissue under my hands. She is dying until she goes into my picture with me, goes in strong, goes in willingly. And once she is in the picture, she gains peace from it, gains the rock strength, the power.

I was young. I was younger than I had a right to be. I was drawn the way a deer is drawn into the halogen lamplight, curious and calm. Heart about to explode. I wasn't helpless, though, not me. I had pictures.

"Show me what you did," Stan said that night, once Ed's mother was resting calmly.

We went into the room at the Red Lion that was Stan's, all carpet and deodorizer. All flocked paper on the walls. Black-red. Gold. Hilarious. Stan lay down on the king-size bed and patted the broad space beside him in a curious, not sexual, way. I lay down there and closed my eyes.

"Show me Milwaukee," Stan whispered. I breathed deep and let out the hems of my thoughts. After a while, then, I got the heft of it, the green medians in June, the way you felt entering your favorite restaurant with a dinner reservation, hungry, knowing that within fifteen minutes German food would start to fill you, German bread, German beer, German schnitzel. I got the neighborhood where Stan had lived, the powdery stucco, the old-board rotting infrastructure and the back yard, all shattered sun and shade, leaves; got Stan's mother lying on the ground full-length in a red suit, asleep; got the back porch, full of suppressed heat; and got the june bugs razzing indomitable against the night screens. Got the smell of Stan's river, got the first-day-of-school smell, the chalk and wax, the cleaned-and-stored, paper-towel scent of Milwaukee schools in the beginning of September. Got the milk cartons, got the straws. Got Stan's brother, thin and wiry arms holding Stan down. Got Stan a hot-dog stand, a nickel bag of peanuts, thirst.

"No," Stan said. "No more."

He could feel it coming, though I avoided it. I steered away from the burning welts, the scissors, pinched nerves, the dead eye, the strap, the belt, the spike-heeled shoe, the razor, the boiling-hot spilled tapioca, the shards of glass, the knives, the chinked armor, the small sister, the small sister, the basement, anything underground.

"Enough." Stan turned to me.

He didn't know what he wanted to see, and I don't mean to imply that he would see the whole of my picture anyway. I would walk the edge of his picture, and he'd walk the edge of mine, get the crumbs, the drops of water that flew off when a bird shook its feathers. That's how much I got across, but that was all it took. When you share like that, the rest of the earth shuts. You are locked in, twisted close, braided, born.

He smoothed his hands across my hair and closed me against him, and then we shut the door to everything and everyone but us. He stood me next to the bed, took off my clothing piece by piece, and made me climax just by brushing me, slowly, here, there, just by barely touching me until he forced apart my legs and put his mouth on me hard. Stood up. He came into me without a sound. I cried out. He pushed harder and then withdrew. It took more than an hour, by the bedside clock. It took a long time. He held my wrists behind my back and forced me down onto the carpet. Then he bent over me and gently, fast and slow, helplessly, without end or beginning, he went in and out until I grew bored, until I wanted to sleep, until I moaned, until I cried out, until I wanted nothing else, until I wanted him the way I always would from then on, since that first dry summer.

From *The Atlantic Monthly* 280, no. 2 (August 1997): 64-68.
Copyright © Louise Erdrich. Reprinted by permission.

Guides to Reflection

1. In one section of the story, Erdrich's narrator includes a version of Stan's sermon, quoting part of it directly and summarizing the rest. Examine both the sermon's content and the rhetorical strategies Stan uses. What makes his sermon effective?

2. In his sermon, Stan likens Lucifer to "the hijacker of a planet" *(Reader, 119)*. Comment on the usefulness of this image for communicating the nature of evil.

3. Erdrich's central character in the story, a sixteen-year-old girl, has developed a way of psychologically removing herself from her parents' acrimonious fights by imagining pictures of idyllic natural settings. Consider how Erdrich presents this ability in the story. Does she seem to see it as a good thing?

4. At the start of the story Erdrich describes the Montana landscape in which the story takes place. How does the landscape reflect the themes of the story?

7

Tess Gallagher

There is hardly a literary genre Tess Gallagher has not made her own: poetry (her first calling), fiction, essays and art criticism, translation, travel writing, theater and screen plays. Although her range of literary and geographical reference is also wide, ranging from present day Ireland to ancient China, Gallagher's imagination is rooted in the Pacific Northwest, the region where she grew up and continues to live. Whether writing a lyric poem or a short story, she draws on a fund of imagery based on a singular landscape: the great forests that her father worked as a logger, the sea, the expanse of the night sky, the life of bears and hummingbirds, the stories passed down both by native Americans and by Western settlers. And yet, for all this looking outward, her region is as much the human heart—the tangle of human relationships that is as dense as any forest, as deep and volatile as the ocean.

This is not to say that her characters strike the reader as profound or their worlds as mysterious. We see them in beauty salons and in barrooms, mowing a neighbor's lawn or caught up in the quick fire of a supermarket-checkout brawl. The context is usually prosaic: the cast of characters typically men down on their luck and women dealing with real or imagined betrayal. Invariably, however, Gallagher catches us off guard with a shift in tone, a sudden move into the lyrical or the fantastic that takes the reader into new territory. Her 1997 collection of stories, *At the Owl Woman Saloon,* is full of such discoveries, many of them entailing marvelous reversals of expectation. In "Coming and Going," a widow's pathetic situation all but calls forth tears of grief yet generates instead a wry smile. In "A Glimpse of the Buddha," a gutted fish gives up a vision of beauty: a "silken cache of unearthly orange eggs…packed like miniature planets in their translucent sack."[1] In "Rain Flooding Your Campfire," a blind man spends the night "looking" rapturously at stars that someone with full sight has described in vivid detail. Usually located at the end of the story, these arresting images, and the humor that often goes with them, reveal a world we only thought we had figured out.

Tess Gallagher is known not only for her own work, but also for her profound involvement with her late husband, Raymond Carver, one of the great short story writers of the century. The two share a working-class background, a regional mix of middle South and the Pacific Northwest, and characters that belong to the same socioeconomic "place." A forthcoming collection of interviews, letters, and introductions—*Soul Barnacles: The Literature of a Relationship*—will explore something of what Gallagher has called the couple's "luminous reciprocity." During the decade the two shared together, they fostered one another's writing both as muse and critic. This double role encouraged Carver to pursue his poetry and Gallagher to renew her commitment to prose. Since Carver's death in 1988, their mutual interdependence has increasingly become known. One of his most renowned stories, "Cathedral," tells of the impact a blind man has when he comes to visit an old friend and her disgruntled male companion (who becomes the narrator of the tale). The situation was actually based on Gallagher's experience. She first edited Carver's narrative, and then went on to publish her own account of the experience (narrated in a feminine voice) titled "Rain Flooding Your Campfire" in *At the Owl Woman Saloon*. According to Gallagher, "My story became its own story, but it was also in dialogue with his. Literature isn't a closed circuit. It's a universe of intersecting dialogues."[2]

The "intersection of dialogues" provides us with a fit description not only of how Carver and Gallagher sparked off each other, but of how so many of her stories move—from separation to intersection. There are exceptions to this rule, as in "A Box of Rocks," where a wronged sister refuses to reconcile, and her unwitting husband in confusion plays his own part in maintaining a "fixed, irrevocable, closed" situation.[3] However, Gallagher's stories mostly hint at, if not actually describe, reconciliation. A rift between cousins in "The Mother Thief" is healed over Sunday breakfast, "as if a seemingly irresolvable pain had unexpectedly made a bridge for them to cross back toward each other."[4] A flare-up at the cash register in "A Glimpse of the Buddha" ends neither in an argument won nor a peace shared. Still, between two women who are completely unknown to one another before the flare-up, there is nonetheless "a pure and open current,"[5] some unfathomable connection. The victim in this encounter wonders what it would mean to "do unto others" in such a circumstance; she even considers that the "crazy blonde woman" at the checkout represents, however perversely and provocatively, "worthiness in some yet-to-be-recognized form."[6] Could the mad woman be a god in disguise?

Although Christianity is part of Gallagher's cultural inheritance, it does not often enter into her foreground. An exception to this rule is "The Woman Who Prayed," the final story in *At the Owl Woman Saloon*. Its opening describes a situation Gallagher often explores: the loss of innocence in a discovery of betrayal. A girlhood rivalry starts up again when Dotty Lloyd, coming upon a cache of love letters, learns that Hilda Queener is carrying on an affair with her husband Del. She fantasizes the other woman's destruction "with a box of matches and a bottle of kerosene"; she begins to burn the letters, one by one; she says nothing when the leader of her church fellowship group asks her point blank, "Now is there anything we can do for you?" Yet the notion of praying does take root—as a way of "spreading God's presence" (she recalls a pastor's sermon), and "without ceasing" (as Paul said in 1 Thessalonians 5:17). Soon she can do little else, although her prayers—first, on behalf of politicians she has only seen on TV, and then for people and pets she knows—fall on the "unbroken silence of God." Still, she continues until prayer becomes her way of life, as "tidal and vast" as the ocean "going out across the planet, touching for all, pleading for all."

Peter S. Hawkins

Notes

1. Tess Gallagher, *At the Owl Woman Saloon* (New York: Scribner, 1977), 198.
2. William L. Stull and Maureen P. Carroll, "Two Darings," *Philosophy and Literature* 22, no. 2 (October 1998): 475-476.
3. Gallagher, *At the Owl Woman Saloon,* 113.
4. Ibid., 188.
5. Ibid., 198.
6. Ibid., 193.

The Woman Who Prayed

Dotty Lloyd believed herself happily married to a rural mailman named Del—until she came across a cache of love letters from Hilda Queener. It so happened, only the day before, Hilda's poodle had become overexcited and piddled all over the waiting-room couch at the Lady Fox Pet Boutique where Dotty worked.

The instant Dotty discovered Hilda had penned the hidden letters, a memory of a distasteful childhood encounter sprang to mind. Hilda, the daughter of a dentist, had carried herself in junior high with the cool poise of a giraffe at a kite convention. She smelled of Jergens lotion and she was fond of cherry-flavored Life Savers which she shared with her friends. Dotty's father owned and operated the only pest-control service in the town. She gave off the pungent odor of chemicals designed to eradicate.

Nearly thirty years had passed since the two had tangled in eighth grade over Roger Gillwater. Hilda, with great gusto, had slapped Dotty's face in front of their class because Roger had dared to walk Dotty home. In Hilda's mind, Roger was reserved for Hilda. Luckily for him, after high school he'd migrated to Hawaii, where he married a part owner of a beach-side hotel. He had appeared the previous year at their twenty-fifth class reunion wearing leis of lavender orchids and had twice excused himself from his wife to dance with Dotty. On their second foray onto the dance floor, Hilda floated by on a slow number with a grade school principal, and reached over playfully to pick a blossom from one of the leis around Roger's neck. Then the principal's shoulder carried away her knowing smile.

As Dotty now turned one of the letters in her hands, Hilda's jealous slap lashed her cheek across time and space like a one-winged bird. There in the garage, the stunned faces of her adolescent classmates came back to her. They seemed to lean with her over her unfortunate find. The letters had been mailed to Del at P.O. Box 1422. "Queenie," they were signed. "Love, Queenie." Dotty began to check their postmarks to determine the extent and timing of her husband's betrayal. She assumed this was the feared midlife crisis that caused a man in his forties to veer off in search of the "absolute cheese," as one of her customers had put it.

It was scalding in those initial moments to note that the letters had been carefully arranged in the order Del had received them. She saw with chagrin that the top one was dated only three days earlier. Furthermore, the correspondence spanned an entire year and each month's bundle was secured with a wide rubber band, the kind Del used on his mail route. Clearly the letters had been treasured.

She might never have come across them if she hadn't made that foray into the garage to the paint and polish shelves. Dotty had decided to resurrect a scuffed ivory purse for the spring wedding of a niece, and the cardboard box marked "Smoke Detector" had attracted her attention.

Her initial shock was followed quickly by outrage. She fell upon the contents like a lioness onto the carcass of an antelope on the wide Serengeti. She carried the box into the bicycle shed at the back of the house and plugged in an electric heater to ward off the spring damp. After securing the foot stand on her bicycle, she climbed onto the seat to be closer to the lightbulb. There she began to read. Her eyes and heart moved through the pages—hours and days of events of which she'd known nothing.

"My darling, Del,"—the letters often began. Dotty never addressed Del as her "darling." It was a word she considered definitely over the mark. Though they'd been passionate in their twenties, they'd developed a kindly, affectionate intimacy over the years. Sweetie she called him and Sugar. He called her Pumpkin.

She pored through the contents of the letters. The light of the bare electric bulb emphasized the surreptitious nature of her inquiry. "Oh Del, I can hardly bear to know you are so close, yet so far." The expressions, though sickeningly pitched at the level of soap opera, still had the power to wring her heart. Weren't these the very things illicit lovers *always* said?

After the ache died back, though, Hilda's spasmodically expressed longing for Del strangely began to relieve Dotty. She considered it evidence of her husband's care in not meeting her childhood rival too often. He clearly did not want to arouse suspicion and bring on the collapse of their marriage. Or was she grasping at straws? No sooner had she been able to shore herself up than she would read from Hilda: "Your letters are a great comfort to me." Just to imagine love letters from Del, nestled among lingerie from Frederick's of Hollywood in Hilda's bureau across town, made Dotty fairly steam. She and Del had courted beginning in high school, so they hadn't needed love letters. She felt retroactively robbed! She wanted to drive to Hilda's with a box of matches and a barrel of kerosene.

Instead, she took the letters from the box, hid them under a sack of birdseed, and unplugged the heater. Then she returned the box to the garage shelf and made straight for the beach down the hill. It was Wednesday, her one afternoon off. She needed to get hold of herself before Del came home at five.

Like the ocean before her, Dotty's mind began to move in and out over her dilemma. She noticed that the ocean no longer consoled her. It instead presented itself as a huge methodical system which mulled and combed and splashed itself from time to time. It simply claimed, then retracted; mulled, then recoiled. With the tide frothing toward the white logs marooned on the beach, she made the decision not to confront Del with what she'd found until she was ready.

Somehow she got through the evening without bursting into tears or saying anything sharp or insinuating to Del. They watched a program on an archaeological dig somewhere in the Middle East, had a snack of cantaloupe, and went to bed. Lying next to Del, knowing about the letters, caused her to feel more alone than she could recall. She turned away from him, drawing her knees up inside her gown. Just as she dropped into sleep, Hilda Queener whirled past with one of Roger Gillwater's leis garlanding her long neck.

At her job next morning, a feeling of counterfeit normalcy returned. She ran shears over Bucky, a black cocker spaniel, and considered how to bring up the subject of the letters to Del. She feared she would accuse, berate, and condemn. And why not? He had to answer for what he was doing. Yet even to speak of this would involve such a departure from the safe shore of their mutual respect and kindliness that the prospect overwhelmed her. She knew that once she told Del of her discovery, Hilda would take center stage. As long as Dotty kept things to herself, in a way the betrayal hadn't quite happened. The secret of her discovery matched the secret of the affair.

It seemed prophetic that she was working on Bucky as she addressed her quandary. The dog, named after Buckminster Fuller, lay on its side with the plaintive whites of its eyes showing. Bucky had been saved by an architect just prior to his scheduled execution at the pound. Dotty ran the electric clippers carefully along one black velvet ear cradled over her palm. When she stared into those brown eyes she thought she glimpsed a kindred soul. The animal seemed to beseech, to ask perpetually to be spared. She wanted as much.

That night after dinner their church fellowship group arrived at the house for their scheduled "visiting night." After reading and discussing Scripture together, it was customary, at the end of such visits, to ask the householders if they would like to discuss any personal trouble. Dotty felt herself trembling when Ms. Carriveau, the feisty group leader, asked, "Now, is there anything we can do for *you?*" Dotty looked toward Del, but his head was already bowed in preparation for the closing words. They all joined hands and Ginger Carriveau gave a blanket, all-purpose prayer. Dotty was grateful to shut her eyes and bow her own head, not to have to look at Del, who showed not a trace of remorse or guilt.

Inside the calm space of prayer, Dotty felt comforted. She'd always prayed at the usual times and places. But this time the benevolent, concentrated force she'd been closing her eyes toward since childhood seemed to have been patiently awaiting her. As she prayed now, in the secret pain of her discovery, the letters seemed to shed some of their power, to recede from the infectious claim they'd begun to make on her life.

May you, Del and Dotty, trust in each other, and in God's will. Let His guidance come into your hearts. Amen," Ginger said confidently, as if, by expressing this aloud, it was sure to happen. They continued in silence for a few moments, as was their custom, offering their private prayers. Del's palm clasped Dotty's in seemingly perfect agreement to their life together. How dear he was, despite all. It was hard to believe he could be apart from her, straying with the likes of the twice-divorced Hilda Queener.

After the members of the fellowship group shook hands and headed to their cars, Dotty turned and gazed at Del. He had the untarnished look of a pilgrim in frontier portraits of the first Thanksgiving. His mild blue eyes, set deeply below his high forehead, belied her recent discovery.

During the rest of the evening they were tender with each other and she had the strong impulse to reveal that she'd found the letters. But the urge gave way to wanting to visit the letters once again, alone. Inside the prayer, Dotty had been able to feel *she,* not the letters, held the power. The fact that she could let this trouble drift offshore for a time, without addressing it, gave her hope that her relationship with Del was durable, resilient enough to withstand whatever might come. Even this. There was no reason to hurry. That had been the lasting message of the waves as she'd walked the day before.

Later that night, while Del was showering, she decided to make a trip to the bicycle shed. She picked up a box of wooden matches from the counter and took a saucepan from the cupboard. Once inside the shed, she put the pan and matches down, took up one of the recent letters and climbed, like a schoolgirl, onto the unsteady perch of her bicycle. She read the letter in its entirety. Hilda Queener provided the sorts of details she could not banish— that she wore Del's flannel shirt to bed, a shirt he'd left with her for that purpose. Hilda wrote she was "putting aside a little spare cash" for them "to take a cozy holiday together." Dotty nearly flew apart at the word "cozy." The last holiday she and Del had taken, the previous summer, they'd pulled their camper near LaPush, sixty miles west, and parked in a clear-cut overlooking the ocean. Dotty read on, bracing herself. Hilda said she was keeping the money in a jar under the sink. "When can you get away?" she asked—as if Del were held prisoner in his own home!

Dotty stepped down from the bicycle and picked up the box of matches. She took one out and ran it along the pebbled side of the box until the head snapped and darted into the flame. As she knelt over the saucepan, she took up the letter and held the match to it. In the relative darkness of the window-less shed the letter, with Hilda's handwriting across its pages, caught fire and seemed to rush upward, assuming heat and power in the small space. The eagerness of the love letter to burn caused her to open her mouth like a child before summer bonfires at the beach. Was she imagining it, or did the pages seem more free, more ardent as they burned? She held page after page of the letter as it lifted into the dark. She hated the letter's agreement to its destruction, its lack of shame. "The hussy!" she said, and heard her mother's voice echo inside her own, as she'd castigated women who "shacked up" rather than marry.

The final bits of paper, tinged with blue, dropped into the saucepan where they smoldered and blackened. She felt mixed about what she'd done. It seemed entirely within her rights, yet, at the same time, she knew it was a weakness to have gone so far. She recalled a story from one of her customers, the owner of a German shepherd with hip trouble. This woman had discovered a single love letter hidden in her husband's fishing-tackle box, next to a Blue Devil lure. She'd waited until he was in the shower to confront him. Then she'd insisted he stay buck-naked, water trickling down his body like sweat, and burn the letter over the toilet, in front of her, to prove that, as he insisted, the woman meant nothing to him. *This*, Dotty had felt, was going too far.

She glanced at the remaining packets. They defied her to consign them to ashes and, for the time being, won a reprieve. She picked up the saucepan and matches and started to the house, pausing to knock the ashes into the brambles.

It was quiet in the house as she entered. She turned the deadbolt and saw that the lights were off in the den. Del had evidently gone to bed. She sat down in the darkened living room and gazed into the yard, lit only by their neighbor's house lights. She had come a long way from the relief and comfort of the prayer earlier that evening. She smelled of smoke, of hidden love, of secrets and betrayal.

The next morning after Del left for the post office she walked out into their yard in her bathrobe. She was working afternoons the rest of the week and she was glad for some time alone. At the base of the apple tee she noticed the faint green-yellow buds of daffodils pursed on the verge of opening. A wren was splashing in the hanging birdbath of the Japanese plum. The scene was guileless, bathed in sunlight. Like a stranger to her own life, she stood in their yard with bounty all around her, and allowed herself a strange impulse. She bowed her head. After a few moments with her eyes closed she felt she'd stepped outside time. Her spirit reeled forth into a vastness that had been there all the time, but which she approached now out of her own direct need. Her attention seemed sturdy and calculated to let any attending powers know she appreciated all she'd been given, despite this recent trouble. She gave thanks for the assurance beauty itself was in the world—that there was a vibrant stir of aliveness of which she was a part, however small.

When she opened her yes, she saw her home with Del afresh—the swing set they'd painted together, the mailbox with their names: "Del and Dot Lloyd" lettered in gold and black, the hummingbird feeder wired to a post near the red-currant bush where the birds would be sure to find it when they returned from their winter migration.

Her uplift in spirit caused her to recall something their pastor had said recently in a sermon: "Prayer is a way of spreading God's presence. As Paul said, 'Pray without ceasing.'" So, perhaps it followed that the more a person prayed, the more God would indeed exist in the world. And the more of God there was in the world, the more banished would be the likes of Hilda Queener—for she knew from living in the same town all these years that Hilda's amorous exertions had caused more than one marriage to ricochet out of orbit. Prayer or no prayer, she couldn't get Hilda out of the picture.

For the next several nights she burned letters over the saucepan. When the last one had crumbled into a gray ash, she realized she knew something she couldn't have known any other way. She hadn't changed anything between Del and Hilda, or between Del and herself, but she had fruitfully crossed and recrossed the boundary between outright anger and aching dismay. Pain had a way of cauterizing itself, she knew, if you could stand it, or stand up to it.

She began to pray in odd moments during her days at the Lady Fox as she groomed a steady succession of animals. She knew it was wrong to ask for things out of selfish motives, but she brazened away, inwardly, and asked that Hilda Queener suffer some debilitation. Nothing life-threatening, mind you. Only purely cosmetic manifestations, such as the sudden release of foul odors, or perhaps if her gums could show when she laughed, or a craving for raw garlic might overtake her. Then Dotty quickly tried to make up for this by praying for refugees in war-torn corners of the world.

After grooming two paired Pekingese and later an Afghan, she went for a break in the little outside snack area. But the prayers wouldn't stop coming. She bowed her head for Hillary Rodham Clinton, who'd been relentlessly under attack. Then she prayed for Robert Dole's crippled arm, his hand carrying the pen with which he would never write illicitly, she felt sure, to any woman across town, or even across the nation, for that matter. She tossed in Newt Gingrich out of concern for what she assumed an apoplectic disposition. Since she was herself a Democrat and a woman, she doubted God's investment in the current ascendant breed of Republican—though, as with other wayward souls she assumed the heavenly door might be left ajar for them to repent and be brought into the fold at some later time. She offered these political prayers in good faith, knowing they might do no more than ripple the surface of her own soul as they wafted off into the universe. But wasn't this the sure good of prayer, that it boomeranged back toward the one who prayed and gave a modicum of hope?

Dotty's boss, Julie, came outside to smoke and found her standing under the maple with her eyes closed.

"Just taking some sun," Dotty said, and did not open her eyes. Julie puffed on her cigarette in silence for a while downwind of Dotty, making curt little snapping noises when her lips left the cigarette. The smoke had a heady, narcotic effect, reminding Dotty of the charred but mentally resilient love letters.

"My hands are itching like crazy," Julie said. "I swear that shampoo leaks right through my rubber gloves!" she complained.

"Uh-huh," Dotty said, and kept on with her prayer for the owner of the Afghan, Cara Jensen, who'd just been told she was out of remission on her breast cancer. Cara had long ago told Dotty that her name in Italian meant "dear one." "Take care, dear Lord, of your dear one, Cara," Dotty prayed.

After Julie went inside, Dotty gave a prayer for Julie's red, chemically scalded hands, so like her own. Then she moved quickly to ask for blessings on a dog named Zowie she'd read about in the morning paper. The animal had been shot and killed protecting its master's home from intruders. She didn't want to neglect this innocent, sacrificed in the line of duty. Its homebound fate was somehow very moving to her.

That night Dotty was gazing out the window as Del drove his pickup into the garage. She heard the truck door slam, but he did not enter the house immediately. She thought of the empty box on the shelf and wondered if he was going to it now, intending to add yet another letter from Hilda, but discovering the others missing.

These thoughts accompanied her present endeavor to keep her mind inside a stream of prayerful reverie she'd entered near the end of her shift at the Lady Fox. She had begun to pray with her eyes open. This allowed her continuous access to her prayers. Dotty had offered so many prayers that day that, if her efforts counted for anything, she was convinced God must be more amply present in the world. Certainly she felt deeply infused by her own attentiveness to those for whom she prayed.

When Del came into the house he said nothing to indicate any change, and they set about fixing a little dinner together of spaghetti and fresh salad. He behaved in a very deferential way to Dotty, as if trying to make something up to her, without revealing what it was. If he had discovered the letters missing, he also had chosen silence.

That night Dotty prayed in the shower and while brushing her teeth—for the sound of running water acted as a natural stimulant to prayer. The longer she kept the secret of the letters, the more the scope of her prayerfulness widened. Virtually every waking moment was spent addressing herself to her prayers. They allowed her to lift away from Del's affair, to bypass it, to ward it off with a genuine and specific concern for others.

As soon as she'd completed one prayer, another suggested itself. She realized how busy the nuns and monks must have been for centuries in their monasteries. She had dearly underestimated them. Each day, when her customers told her of this or that calamity, she set to work. She kept God busy. *She* was busy.

That night in bed, trying to move into sleep, she continued to pray, as if all would be lost if she ceased to perform her repeated pleas. When she tried to regard her effort as possibly hopeless—a silly waste of time—something strong and resilient flared up against her doubt. Del was turned on his side, away from her, but she was aware of his sleeping head on the pillow next to hers. Possibly filled with dreams of Hilda. She couldn't know. For her own part she lay throughout the night in a prayerful drowse that carried her into morning.

When she got out of bed and went downstairs, she saw that Del had already left for work. She was struck by his having gone from the house without waking her. This was unlike him, and unlike her not to have woken. She recalled the moment from past mornings when, after breakfasting together, they kissed good-bye at the door, that island of once harmless departure which had become so bittersweet of late. She saw that his lunch box was missing and that the mayonnaise had been left with its lid off where he'd made his sandwiches. Why this should have caused her to tremble and move toward tears, she didn't know. When she finally quieted herself, she had the urge to pray for something momentous—for Lebanese refugees, for the bereaved relatives of airline passengers lost in a Florida swamp; for anyone, anywhere betrayed, bereft, and lonely. She fit a votive candle on a side table near the couch in the living room and got down before it on her knees.

In some paralysis of her own needs, she focused on the fate of her marriage and on her love for Del. Treacherous or not, he was still her husband, and she'd made all kinds of allowances for him because of what she knew of the wiles of Hilda Queener. She closed her eyes and entered a long, narrow corridor of necessity. She was praying for herself. She was unsure, as with the whole idea of prayer, whether or not her effort was wasted. God could fail to hear or to answer. She might lose her husband to Hilda. But there was something worse than losing Del. She might plunge into a life of doubt and bitter inward-gazing while she raked her soul hopelessly across the unbroken silence of God.

The world felt more intimate there on her knees. The candle flickered and dodged across her face in the daylight. After a while she relaxed into her own love letter, a prayer which issued from her as naturally and needfully as breath. It was intoxicating, like the smell of seaweed—tidal and vast, going out across the planet, touching all, pleading for all.

Prayer unceasing kept her on her knees until the dark came down. It was late when Del returned home. She was aware when he parked in the garage and entered the silent house. A door closed as he crossed into the adjoining room on his way to her. Finally he was over her and she felt him lifting her from her knees by one arm. Then his voice, low and halting, from a distance, as he began to try to explain.

From *At the Owl Woman Saloon* by Tess Gallagher. Copyright © 1997 by Tess Gallagher. Reprinted by permission of Scribner, a division of Simon & Schuster, Inc. and ICM.

Guides to Reflection

1. Critics have observed that on the surface Gallagher's poetry often seems little more than observations about ordinary events or experience, but that when plumbed, it transforms the mundane, and transcends the limits it has worked within. Would such an evaluation fit "The Woman Who Prayed"? How does the ordinary (a girlhood rivalry, a discovered infidelity) open up the heights and depths of human life?

2. The circumstances of the story—a discovered adultery—might easily have led Gallagher to avoid the humor that is in fact at play throughout the story. Yet the setting of Dotty's workplace (the "Lady Fox Pet Boutique"), her catty remarks about Hilda, and the running observations made by and about her—"the sound of running water acted as a natural stimulant to prayer" *(Reader, 135)*—are all undeniably funny. What is the effect of the story's light tone?

3. After her initial discovery of Del's love letters, Dotty goes to the ocean in search of some consolation. Instead, the sea "presented itself as a huge methodical system which mulled and combed and splashed itself from time to time." *(Reader, 130)* By the end of the story, however, we are told that her prayer had taken on the smell of seaweed, and that, like the sea, it was "touching all, pleading for all" *(Reader, 136)*. No longer a "methodical system," the ocean becomes a universal embrace. What is suggested by this change of metaphor and association?

4. What happens to Dotty as she becomes a woman who prays?

5. Discuss your own experience of prayer, particularly insofar as you have known it to "spread God's presence."

8

Tillie Olsen

In the mid-1950s, Tillie Olsen began writing short stories. As a 40-year-old high school dropout, mother of four daughters, labor activist, and itinerant worker, Olsen did not have the sort of education or position one might suppose would characterize the writer of stories that would garner praise from established writers and critics. Yet Olsen was quickly recognized as a significant new voice in American literature, a judgment sustained by subsequent decades. Author Alice Walker has described Olsen as "a writer of such generosity and honesty, she literally saves lives."[1] Summarizing response to Olsen, novelist Margaret Atwood wrote: " 'respect' is too pale a word: 'reverence' is more like it."[2] The Harvard psychiatrist and critic Robert Coles observed of Olsen that "Everything she has written has become almost immediately a classic" and noted that "hers is a singular talent that will not let go of one."[3]

Olsen's art reflects her experience. Born in 1912 or 1913 in Nebraska, Olsen is the daughter of Russian parents who fled to America after participating in a failed revolution against the czar in 1905. Olsen was raised in a poor, racially-mixed neighborhood in Omaha, where her father held a succession of low-paying jobs. Although Olsen attended an academically rigorous high school, she dropped out before graduating so that she could help support her family.

Olsen's parents remained politically active after their immigration to the United States. Olsen's father was for many years the secretary of the Socialist Party in Nebraska. He worked with union organizers in meatpacking plants, and participated in relief efforts for African Americans whose homes and businesses were damaged or destroyed in race riots.

Like her parents, Olsen was politically active. In the 1930s, she was jailed for union activities, first in Kansas City where she had handed out leaflets for the Young Communist League at a meat-packing plant, and again in San Francisco where she participated in a march after two longshoremen were killed in an encounter with police during a strike. During the late 1930s and part of the 1940s Olsen belonged to the Communist party, as did her husband, Jack Olsen. Although Olsen left the party because she was disturbed by its policies and practices, she and her husband struggled to keep jobs during the McCarthy era. Jack Olsen was subpoenaed by and testified before the House Un-American Activities Committee.[4]

Throughout her adult life, Olsen has been particularly interested in social and political issues relating to women. Her first published work, a poem in the March 1934 issue of *The Partisan Review,* depicts the cruel conditions in which women worked in the garment industry. An early novel, *Yonnodio,* depicts the hardships endured by women during the Depression. Most significantly, *Silences* (1978) raised public awareness of the challenges women writers have encountered. A compilation of lectures, essays, quotations, and statistics, *Silences* reports that in the early 1970s men wrote 94 percent of works studied in college literature courses. Of 90 literature textbooks Olsen examined, 12 included no women writers at all, even though from 1919 to 1973 nearly 17 percent of literary prize winners were women.[5] Olsen's analysis and her eloquent pleas for change have been important elements of the feminist movement in academia, which has significantly changed schools and colleges since the 1970s.

While Olsen's political and social activism seems a clear inheritance from her parents, her attitudes toward religion seem rather different. According to Olsen, her parents were atheists. Olsen's father was born to a Jewish family, as her mother probably was also.[6] Olsen has said of her mother that "As a girl in long ago Czarist Russia, she had sternly broken with all observances of organized religion, associating it with pogroms and wars; 'mind forg'd manacles'; a repressive state."[7] But Olsen's parents must have tolerated her exploration of religious belief and experience because Olsen began at age nine or ten attending Calvary Baptist Church, a black church close to her home in Omaha, where she sang in a choir. After she moved to San Francisco as an adult, Olsen occasionally attended church with a black friend and sang in a choir. Olsen has described the churches she attended as categorically different from the organized religion her parents had known. She has praised these churches, which minister to

> not only the hunger of people for a place where they feel they belong and are treated with dignity but the special character of black churches and the other churches that *are* people's solace, source of community, source of strength and keep alive the human spirit of resistance, of deeply felt song, of joy. What was the basic institution that made the Civil Rights movement, the human rights movement possible? Where was its major fortress? The churches, the black churches.[8]

Olsen credits her experiences over many years in black churches with giving her a sense of the power and value religious belief can have.

The work that most directly shows the influence of Olsen's attendance at black churches is her story "O Yes," published first in 1957 with the title "Baptism" and then included in the collection *Tell Me a Riddle* (1961). In this story, a 12-year-old white girl, Carol, goes to a black church for the baptism of her former best friend, Parry. Olsen depicts the church as a place filled with color, light, vibrancy, and song. Both the minister's sermon and the hymns the congregation sings portray God as a powerful redeemer who brings hope and finally salvation to those who suffer in the "sea of trouble" *(Reader, 147)* that life often is for the parishioners. The troubles of the world loom large for Carol at the church service because she acutely feels her otherness. Now a student in junior high school, she finds it hard to sustain her friendship with Parry. Social pressures push them into separate groups marked by race and class boundaries. Stunned by the ecstatic religious experience of the people in church and fearful of being seen by black students from her school, Carol collapses and must leave the church.

In the second part of "O Yes," Olsen depicts the anguish of Carol and her family as they struggle to understand and resist the strong social forces that threaten to shape their lives in ways that seem false and cruel. Parry's visit to Carol, sick with the mumps, shows the pain of what Carol's sister calls "sorting" and leaves Carol shaken. Carol's mother, Helen, cannot find words to console Carol, and at the end of the story she too feels bereft, longing for things to be different.

Olsen does not leave her characters in despair. The anguish and fear are strong. Carol's piercing cry, "Oh why is it like it is and why do I have to care?" *(Reader, 155)*, reverberates sorrowfully at the end of the story, but the fact that she does empathize, that she does care, offers hope. And Helen's memory of the parishioners at Parry's church reminds us of a community that can be "a place of strength" *(Reader, 155)* that both challenges the restricting and cruel structures of society and also promises understanding, support, and love.

Paula J. Carlson

Notes

1. Alice Walker, *In Search of Our Mothers' Gardens* (New York: Harcourt Brace, 1983), 14.
2. Margaret Atwood, "Obstacle Course," *New York Times Book Review* (30 July 1978): 1.
3. Robert Coles, "Reconsideration," *The New Republic* (6 Dec. 1975): 30.
4. Mickey Pearlman and Abby H. P. Werlock, *Tillie Olsen* (Boston: Twayne, 1991), 9-36.
5. Tillie Olsen, *Silences* (New York: Delacorte, 1978), 186-189.
6. Pearlman, 9.
7. Quoted in Joanne S. Frye, *Tillie Olsen: A Study of the Short Fiction* (New York: Twayne, 1995), 77.
8. Quoted in Frye, 160.

O Yes

1

They are the only white people there, sitting in the dimness of the Negro church that had once been a corner store, and all through the bubbling, swelling, seething of before the services, twelve-year-old Carol clenches tight her mother's hand, the other resting lightly on her friend, Parialee Phillips, for whose baptism she has come.

The white-gloved ushers hurry up and down the aisle, beckoning people to their seats. A jostle of people. To the chairs angled to the left for the youth choir, to the chairs angled to the right for the ladies' choir, even up to the platform, where behind the place for the dignitaries and the mixed choir, the new baptismal tank gleams—and as if pouring into it from the ceiling, the blue-painted River of Jordan, God standing in the waters, embracing a brown man in a leopard skin and pointing to the letters of gold:

REJOICE

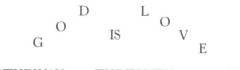

I AM THE WAY   THE TRUTH   THE LIFE

At the clear window, the crucified Christ embroidered on the starched white curtain leaps in the wind of the sudden singing. And the choirs march in. Robes of wine, of blue, of red.

"We stands and sings too," says Parialee's mother, Alva, to Helen; though already Parialee has pulled Carol up. Singing, little Lucinda Phillips fluffs out her many petticoats; singing, little Bubbie bounces up and down on his heels.

> *Any day now I'll reach that land of freedom,*
>> *Yes, o yes*
> *Any day now, know that promised land*

The youth choir claps and taps to accent the swing of it. Beginning to tap, Carol stiffens. "Parry, look. Somebody from school."

"Once more once," says Parialee, in the new way she likes to talk now.

"Eddie Garlin's up there. He's in my math."

"Couple cats from Franklin Jr. chirps in the choir. No harm or alarm."

Anxiously Carol scans the faces to see who else she might know, who else might know her, but looks quickly down to Lucinda's wide skirts, for it seems Eddie looks back at her, sullen or troubled, though it is hard to tell, faced as she is into the window of curtained sunblaze.

> *I know my robe will fit me well*
> *I tried it on at the gates of hell*

If it were a record she would play it over and over, Carol thought, to untwine the intertwined voices, to search how the many rhythms rock apart and yet are one glad rhythm.

> *When I get to heaven gonna sing and shout*
> *Nobody be able to turn me out*

"That's Mr. Chairback Evans going to invocate," Lucinda leans across Parry to explain. "He don't invoke good like Momma."

"Shhhh."

"Momma's the only lady in the church that invocates. She made the prayer last week. (Last month, Lucy.) I made the children's 'nouncement last time. (That was way back Thanksgiving.) And Bubbie's 'nounced too. Lots of times."

"Lucy-inda. SIT!"

Bible study announcements and mixed-choir practice announcements and Teen Age Hearts meeting announcements.

If Eddie said something to her about being there, worried Carol, if he talked to her right in front of somebody at school.

Messengers of Faith announcements and Mamboettes announcement and Committee for the Musical Tea.

Parry's arm so warm. Not realizing, starting up the old game from grade school, drumming a rhythm on the other's arm to see if the song could be guessed. "Parry, guess."

But Parry is pondering the platform.

The baptismal tank? "Parry, are you scared...the baptizing?"

"This cat? No." Shaking her head so slow and scornful, the barrette in her hair, sun fired, strikes a long rail of light. And still ponders the platform.

New Strangers Baptist Church invites you and Canaan Fair Singers announcements and Battle of Song and Cosmopolites meet. "O Lord, I couldn't find no ease," a solo. The ladies' choir:

> O what you say seekers, o what you say seekers,
> Will you never turn back no more?

The mixed choir sings:

> Ezekiel saw that wheel of time
> Every spoke was of humankind...

And the slim worn man in the pin-stripe suit starts his sermon On the Nature of God. How God is long-suffering. Oh, how long he has suffered. Calling the roll of the mighty nations, that rose and fell and now are dust for grinding the face of Man.

O voice of drowsiness and dream to which Carol does not need to listen. As long ago. Parry warm beside her too, as it used to be, there in the class-room at Mann Elementary, and the feel of drenched in sun and dimness and dream. Smell and sound of the chalk wearing itself away to nothing, rustle of books, drumming tattoo of fingers on her arm: *Guess.*

And as the preacher's voice spins happy and free, it is the used-to-be play-yard. Tag. Thump of the volley ball. Ecstasy of the jump rope. Parry, do pepper. Carol, do pepper. Parry's bettern Carol, Carol's bettern Parry....

Did someone scream?

It seemed someone screamed—but all were sitting as before, though the sun no longer blared through the windows. She tried to see up where Eddie was, but the ushers were standing at the head of the aisle now, the ladies in white dresses like nurses or waitresses wear, the men holding their white-gloved hands up so one could see their palms.

"And God is Powerful," the preacher was chanting. "Nothing for him to scoop out the oceans and pat up the mountains. Nothing for him to scoop up the miry clay and create man. Man, I said, create Man."

The lady in front of her moaned *"O yes"* and others were moaning *"O yes."*

"And when the earth mourned the Lord said, Weep not, for all will be returned to you, every dust, every atom. And the tired dust settles back, goes back. Until that Judgment Day. That great day."

"O yes."

The ushers were giving out fans. Carol reached for one and Parry said: "What *you* need one for?" but she took it anyway.

"You think Satchmo can blow; you think Muggsy can blow; you think Dizzy can blow?" He was straining to an imaginary trumpet now, his head far back and his voice coming out like a trumpet.

"Oh Parry, he's so good."

"Well. Jelly jelly."

"Nothing to Gabriel on that great getting-up morning. And the horn wakes up Adam, and Adam runs to wake up Eve, and Eve moans; Just one more minute, let me sleep, and Adam yells, Great Day, woman, don't you know it's the Great Day?"

"Great Day, Great Day," the mixed choir behind the preacher rejoices:

> *When our cares are past*
> *When we're home at last…*

"And Eve runs to wake up Cain." Running round the platform, stooping and shaking imaginary sleepers, "and Cain runs to wake up Abel." Looping, scalloping his voice—"Grea-aaa-aat Daaaay." All the choirs thundering:

> *Great Day*
> *When the battle's fought*
> *And the victory's won*

Exultant spirals of sound. And Carol caught into it (Eddie forgotten, the game forgotten) chanting with Lucy and Bubbie: *"Great Day."*

"Ohhhhhhhhhh," his voice like a trumpet again, "the re-unioning. Ohhhhhhhhh, the rejoicing. After the ages immemorial of longing."

Someone *was* screaming. And an awful thrumming sound with it, like feet and hands thrashing around, like a giant jumping of a rope.

"Great Day." And no one stirred or stared as the ushers brought a little woman out into the aisle, screaming and shaking, just a little shrunk-up woman, not much taller than Carol, the biggest thing about her her swollen hands and the cascades of tears wearing her face.

The shaking inside Carol too. Turning and trembling to ask: "What? … that lady?" But Parry still ponders the platform; little Lucy loops the chain of her bracelet round and round; and Bubbie sits placidly, dreamily. Alva Phillips is up fanning a lady in front of her; two lady ushers are fanning other people Carol cannot see. And her mother, her mother looks in a sleep.

Yes. He raised up the dead from the grave. He made old death behave.

Yes. Yes. From all over, hushed.   *O Yes*

He was your mother's rock. Your father's mighty tower. And he gave us a little baby. A little baby to love.

I am so glad

Yes, your friend, when you're friendless. Your father when you're fatherless.

Way maker. Door opener.

Yes

When it seems you can't go on any longer, he's there. You can, he says, you can.

Yes

And that burden you been carrying—ohhhhh that burden—not for always will it be. No, not for always.

Stay with me, Lord

I will put my Word in you and it is power. I will put my Truth in you and it is power.

O Yes

Out of your suffering I will make you to stand as a stone. A tried stone. Hewn out of the mountains of ages eternal. Ohhhhhhhhhh. Out of the mire I will lift your feet. Your tired feet from so much wandering. From so much work and wear and hard times.

Yes

From so much journeying—and never the promised land. And I'll wash them in the well your tears made. And I'll shod them in the gospel of peace, and of feeling good. Ohhhhhhhhh.

O Yes.

Behind Carol, a trembling wavering scream. Then the thrashing. Up above, the singing:

> *They taken my blessed Jesus and flogged him to the woods*
> *And they made him hew out his cross and they dragged him to Calvary*
> *Shout, brother. Shout shout shout, He never cried a word.*

Powerful throbbing voices. Calling and answering to each other.

> *They taken my blessed Jesus and whipped him up the hill*
> *With a knotty whip and a raggedy thorn he never cried a word.*
> *Shout sister. Shout shout shout. He never cried a word.*
>
> *Go tell the people the Saviour has risen*
> *Has risen from the dead and will live forevermore*
> *And won't have to die no more.*
> *Halleloo.*
> > *Shout, brother, shout*
> > *We won't have to die no more!*

A single exultant lunge of shriek. Then the thrashing. All around a clapping. Shouts with it. The piano whipping, whipping air to a froth. Singing now.

> > *I once was lost who now am found*
> > *Was blind who now can see*

On Carol's fan, a little Jesus walked on wondrously blue waters to where bearded disciples spread nets out of a fishing boat. If she studied the fan—

became it—it make a wall around her. If she could make what was happening (*what* was happening?) into a record small and round to listen to far and far as if into a seashell—the stamp and rills and spirals all tiny (but never any screaming).

wade wade in the water

Jordan's water is chilly and wild
I've got to get home to the other side
God's going to trouble the waters

The music leaps and prowls. Ladders of screamings. Drumming feet of ushers running. And still little Lucy fluffs her skirts, loops the chain on her bracelet; still Bubbie sits and rocks dreamily; and only eyes turn for an instant to the aisle as if nothing were happening. "Mother, let's go home," Carol begs, but her mother holds her so tight. Alva Phillips, strong Alva, rocking too and chanting, *O Yes.* No, do not look.

Wade,
Sea of trouble all mingled with fire
Come on my brethren it's time to go higher
Wade wade

The voices in great humming waves, slow, slow (when did it become the humming?), everyone swaying with it too, moving like in slow waves and singing, and up where Eddie is, a new cry, wild and open, "O help me, Jesus," and when Carol opens her eyes she closes them again, quick, but still can see the new known face from school (not Eddie), the thrashing, writhing body, struggling against the ushers with the look of grave and loving support on their faces, and hear the torn, tearing cry: "Don't take me away, life everlasting, don't take me away."

And now the rhinestones in Parry's hair glitter wicked, the white hands of the ushers, fanning, foam in the air; the blue-painted waters of Jordan swell and thunder; Christ spirals on his cross in the window, and she is drowned under the sluice of the slow singing and the sway.

So high up and forgotten the waves and the world, so stirless the deep cool green and the wrecks of what had been. Here now Hostess Foods, where Alva Phillips works her nights—but different from that time Alva had taken them through before work, for it is all sunken under water, the creaking loading platform where they had left the night behind; the closet room where Alva's swaddles of sweaters, boots, and cap hung, the long hall lined with pickle barrels, the sharp freezer door swinging open.

Bubbles of breath that swell. A gulp of numbing air. She swims into the chill room where the huge wheels of cheese stand, and Alva swims too, deftly oiling each machine: slicers and wedgers and the convey, that at her touch start to roll and grind. The light of day blazes up and Alva is holding a cup, saying: Drink this, baby.

"DRINK IT." Her mother's voice and the numbing air demanding her to pay attention. Up through the waters and into the car.

"That's right, lambie, now lie back." Her mother's lap.

"Mother."

"Shhhhh. You almost fainted, lambie."

Alva's voice. "You gonna be all right, Carol...Lucy, I'm telling you for the last time, you and Buford get back into that church. Carol is *fine*."

"Lucyinda, if I had all your petticoats I could float." Crying. "Why didn't you let me wear my full skirt with the petticoats, Mother."

"Shhhhh, lamb." Smoothing her cheek. "Just breathe, take long deep breaths."

"... How you doing now, you little ol' consolation prize?" It is Parry, but she does not come in the car or reach to Carol through the open window: "No need to cuss and fuss. You going to be sharp as a tack, Jack."

Answering automatically: "And cool as a fool."

Quick, they look at each other.

"Parry, we have to go home now, don't we, Mother? I almost fainted, didn't I, Mother?...Parry, I'm sorry I got sick and have to miss your baptism."

"Don't feel sorry. I'll feel better you not there to watch. It was our mommas wanted you to be there, not me."

"Parry!" Three voices.

"Maybe I'll come over to play kickball after. If you feeling better. Maybe. Or bring the pogo." Old shared joys in her voice. "Or any little thing."

In just a whisper: "Or any little thing. Parry. Good-bye, Parry."

And why does Alva have to talk now?

"You all right? You breathin' deep like your momma said? Was it too close 'n hot in there? Did something scare you, Carrie?"

Shaking her head to lie, "No."

"I blame myself for not paying attention. You not used to people letting go that way. Lucy and Bubbie, Parialee, they used to it. They been coming since they lap babies."

"Alva, that's all right. Alva, Mrs. Phillips."

"You *was* scared. Carol, it's something to study about. You'll feel better if you understand."

Trying not to listen.

"You not used to hearing what people keeps inside, Carol. You know how music can make you feel things? Glad or sad or like you can't sit still? That was religion music, Carol."

"I have to breathe deep, Mother said."

"Not everybody feels religion the same way. Some it's in their mouth, but some it's like a hope in their blood, their bones. And they singing songs every word that's real to them, Carol, every word out of they own life. And the preaching finding lodgment in their hearts."

The screaming was tuning up in her ears again, high above Alva's patient voice and the waves lapping and fretting.

"Maybe somebody's had a hard week, Carol, and they locked up with it. Maybe a lot of hard weeks bearing down."

"Mother, my head hurts."

"And they're home, Carol, church is home. Maybe the only place they can feel how they feel and maybe let it come out. So they can go on. And it's all right."

"Please, Alva. Mother, tell Alva my head hurts."

"Get Happy, we call it, and most it's a good feeling, Carol. When you got all that locked up inside you."

"Tell her we have to go home. It's all right, Alva. Please, Mother. Say good-bye. Good-bye."

When I was carrying Parry and her father left me, and I fifteen years old, one thousand miles away from home, sin-sick and never really believing, as still I don't believe all, scorning, for what have it done to help, waiting there in the clinic and maybe sleeping, a voice called: Alva, Alva. So mournful and so sweet: Alva. Fear not, I have loved you from the foundation of the universe. And a little small child tugged on my dress. He was carrying a parade stick, on the end of it a star that outshined the sun. Follow me, he said. And the real sun went down and he hidden his stick. How dark it was, how dark. I could feel the darkness with my hands. And when I could see, I screamed. Dump trucks run, dumping bodies in hell, and a convey line run, never ceasing with souls, weary ones having to stamp and shove them along, and the air like fire. Oh I never want to hear such screaming. Then the little child jumped on a motorbike making a path no bigger than my little finger. But first he greased my feet with the hands of my momma when I was a knee baby. They shined like the sun was on them. Eyes he placed all around my head, and as I journeyed upward after him, it seemed I heard a mourning: "Mama Mama you must help carry the world." The rise and fall of nations I saw. And the voice called again Alva Alva, and I flew into a world of light, multitudes singing, Free, free, I am so glad.

2

Helen began to cry, telling her husband about it.

"You and Alva ought to have your heads examined, taking her there cold like that," Len said. "All right, wreck my best handkerchief. Anyway, now that she's had a bath, her Sunday dinner…."

"And been fussed over," seventeen-year-old Jeannie put in.

"She seems good as new. Now *you* forget it, Helen."

"I can't. Something…deep happened. If only I or Alva had told her what it would be like…. But I didn't realize."

You don't realize a lot of things, Mother, Jeannie said, but not aloud.

"So Alva talked about it after instead of before. Maybe it meant more that way."

"Oh Len, she didn't listen."

"You don't know if she did or not. Or what there was in the experience for her…."

Enough to pull that kid apart two ways even more, Jeannie said, but still not aloud.

"I was so glad she and Parry were going someplace together again. Now that'll be between them too. Len, they really need, miss each other. What happened in a few months? When I think of how close they were, the hours of makebelieve and dressup and playing ball and collecting…."

"Grow up, Mother." Jeannie's voice was harsh. "Parialee's collecting something else now. Like her own crowd. Like jivetalk and rhythmandblues. Like teachers who treat her like a dummy and white kids who treat her like dirt; boys who think she's really something and chicks who…."

"Jeannie, I know. It hurts."

"Well, maybe it hurts Parry too. Maybe. At least she's got a crowd. Just don't let it hurt Carol though, 'cause there's nothing she can do about it. That's all through, her and Parialee Phillips, put away with their paper dolls."

"No, Jeannie, no."

"It's like Ginger and me. Remember Ginger, my best friend in Horace Mann. But you hardly noticed when it happened to us, did you … because she was white? Yes, Ginger, who's got two kids now, who quit school year before last. Parry's never going to finish either. What's she got to do with Carrie any more? They're going different places. Different places, different crowds. And they're sorting…."

"Now wait, Jeannie. Parry's just as bright, just as capable."

"They're in junior high, Mother. Don't you know about junior high? How they sort? And it's all where you're going. Yes and Parry's colored and Carrie's white. And you have to watch everything, what you wear and how you wear it and who you eat lunch with and how much homework you do and how you act to the teacher and what you laugh at…. And run with your crowd."

"Is that final?" asked Len. "Don't you think kids like Carol and Parry can show it doesn't *have* to be that way."

"They can't. They can't. They don't let you."

"No need to shout," he said mildly. "And who do you mean by 'they' and what do you mean by 'sorting'?"

How they sort. A foreboding of comprehension whirled within Helen. What was it Carol had told her of the Welcome Assembly the first day in junior high? The models showing How to Dress and How Not to Dress and half the girls in their loved new clothes watching their counterparts up on the stage—*their* straight skirt, their sweater, their earrings, lipstick, hairdo—"How Not to Dress," "a bad reputation for your school." It was nowhere in Carol's description, yet picturing it now, it seemed to Helen that a mute cry of violated dignity hung in the air. Later there had been a story of going to another Low 7 homeroom on an errand and seeing a teacher trying to wipe the forbidden lipstick off a girl who was fighting back and cursing. Helen could hear Carol's frightened, self-righteous tones: "...and I hope they expel her; she's the kind that gives Franklin Jr. a bad rep; she doesn't care about anything and always gets into fights." Yet there was nothing in these incidents to touch the heavy comprehension that waited.... Homework, the wonderings those times Jeannie and Carol needed help: "What if there's no one at home to give the help, and the teachers with their two hundred and forty kids a day can't or don't or the kids don't ask and they fall hopelessly behind, what then?"—but this too was unrelated. And what had it been that time about Parry? "Mother, Melanie and Sharon won't go if they know Parry's coming." Then of course you'll go with Parry, she's been your friend longer, she had answered, but where was it they were going and what had finally happened? Len, my head hurts, she felt like saying, in Carol's voice in the car, but Len's eyes were grave on Jeannie who was saying passionately:

"If you think it's so goddam important why do we have to live here where it's for real; why don't we move to Ivy like Betsy (yes, I know, money), where it's the deal to be buddies, in school anyway, three coloured kids and their father's a doctor or judge or something big wheel and one always gets elected President or head song girl or something to prove oh how we're democratic.... What do you want of that poor kid anyway? Make up your mind. Stay friends with Parry—but be one of the kids. Sure. Be a brain—but not a square. Rise on up, college prep, but don't get separated. Yes, stay one of the kids but...."

"Jeannie. You're not talking about Carol at all, are you, Jeannie? Say it again. I wasn't listening. I was trying to think."

"She will not say it again," Len said firmly, "you look about ready to pull a Carol. One a day's our quota. And you, Jeannie, we'd better cool it. Too much to talk about for one session.... Here, come to the window and watch the Carol and Parry you're both all worked up about."

In the wind and the shimmering sunset light, half the children of the block are playing down the street. Leaping, bouncing, hallooing, tugging the kites of spring. In the old synchronized understanding, Carol and Parry kick, catch, kick, catch. And now Parry jumps on her pogo stick (the last time), Carol shadowing her, and Bubbie, arching his body in a semicircle of joy, bounding after them, high, higher, higher.

And the months go by and supposedly it is forgotten, except for the now and then when, self-important, Carol will say: I really truly did nearly faint, didn't I, Mother, that time I went to church with Parry?

And now seldom Parry and Carol walk the hill together. Melanie's mother drives by to pick up Carol, and the several times Helen has suggested Parry, too, Carol is quick to explain: "She's already left" or "She isn't ready; she'll make us late."

And after school? Carol is off to club or skating or library or someone's house, and Parry can stay for kickball only on the rare afternoons when she does not have to hurry home where Lucy, Bubbie, and the cousins wait to be cared for, now Alva works the four to twelve-thirty shift.

No more the bending together over the homework. All semester the teachers have been different, and rarely Parry brings her books home, for where is there space or time and what is the sense? And the phone never rings with: what you going to wear tomorrow, are you bringing your lunch, or come on over, let's design some clothes for the Katy Keane comic-book contest. And Parry never drops by with Alva for Saturday snack to or from grocery shopping.

And the months go by and the sorting goes on and seemingly it is over until that morning when Helen must stay home from work, so swollen and feverish is Carol with mumps.

The afternoon before, Parry had come by, skimming up the stairs, spilling books and binders on the bed: Hey frail, lookahere and wail, your momma askin for homework, what she got against YOU?...looking quickly once then not looking again and talking fast.... Hey, you bloomed. You gonna be your own pumpkin, hallowe'en? Your momma know yet it's mu-umps? And lumps. Momma says: no distress, she'll be by tomorrow morning see do you need anything while your momma's to work.... (Singing: *whole lotta shakin goin on.*) All your 'signments is inside; Miss Rockface says the teachers to write 'em cause I mightn't get it right all right.

But did not tell: Does your mother work for Carol's mother? Oh, you're neighbors! Very well, I'll send along a monitor to open Carol's locker but you're only to take these things I'm writing down, nothing else. Now say after me: Miss Campbell is trusting me to be a good responsible girl. And go right to Carol's house. After school. Not stop anywhere on the way. Not lose anything. And only take. What's written on the list. You really gonna mess with that book stuff? Sign on *mine* says do-not-open-until-eX-mas.... That Mrs. Fernandez doll she didn't send nothin, she was the only, says feel better and read a book to report if you feel like and I'm the most for takin care for you; she's my most, wish I could get her but she only teaches 'celerated.... Flicking the old read books on the shelf but not opening to mock-declaim as once she used to ... Vicky, Eddie's g.f. in Rockface office, she's on suspended for sure, yellin to Rockface: you bitchkitty don't you give me no more bad shit. That Vicky she can sure sling-ating-ring it. Staring out the window as if the tree not there in which they had hid out and rocked so often.... For sure. *(Keep mo-o-vin.)* Got me a new pink top and lilac skirt. Look sharp with this purple? Cinching in the wide belt as if delighted with what newly swelled above and swelled below. Wear it Saturday night to Sweet's, Modernaires Sounds of Joy, Leroy and Ginny and me goin if Momma'll stay home. IF. *(Shake my baby shake.)* How come old folks still likes to party? Huh? Asking of Rembrandt's weary old face looking from the wall. How come (softly) you long-gone you. Touching her face to his quickly, lightly. NEXT mumps is your buddybud Melanie's turn to tote your stuff. *I'm* getting the hoovus goovus. Hey you so unneat, don't care what you bed with. Removing the books and binders, ranging them on the dresser one by one, marking lipstick faces—bemused or mocking or amazed—on each paper jacket. Better. Fluffing out smoothing the quilt with exaggerated energy. Any little thing I can get, cause I gotta blow. Tossing up and catching their year-ago, arm-in-arm graduation picture, replacing it deftly, upside down, into its mirror crevice. Joe. Bring you joy juice or fizz water or kickapoo? Adding a frown line to one bookface. Twanging the paper fishkite, the Japanese windbell overhead, setting the mobile they had once made of painted eggshells and decorated straws to twirling and rocking. And is gone.

She talked to the lipstick faces after, in her fever, tried to stand on her head to match the picture, twirled and twanged with the violent overhead.

Sleeping at last after the disordered night. Having surrounded herself with the furnishings of that world of childhood she no sooner learned to live in comfortably, then had to leave.

The dollhouse stands there to arrange and rearrange; the shell and picture card collections to re-sort and remember; the population of dolls given away to little sister, borrowed back, propped all around to dress and undress and caress.

She has thrown off her nightgown because of the fever, and her just bud-ding breast is exposed where she reaches to hold the floppy plush dog that had been her childhood pillow.

Not for anything would Helen have disturbed her. Except that in the unac-customedness of a morning at home, in the bruised restlessness after the sleepless night, she clicks on the radio—and the storm of singing whirls into the room:

> *... of trouble all mingled with fire*
> *Come on my brethren we've got to go higher*
> *Wade, wade....*

And Carol runs down the stairs, shrieking and shrieking. "Turn it off, Mother, turn it off." Hurling herself at the dial and wrenching it so it comes off in her hand.

"Ohhhhh," choked and convulsive, while Helen tries to hold her, to quiet.

"Mother, why did they sing and scream like that?"

"At Parry's church?"

"Yes." Rocking and strangling the cries. "I hear it all the time." Clinging and beseeching. "...What was it, Mother? Why?"

Emotion, Helen thought of explaining, *a characteristic of the religion of all oppressed peoples, yes your very own great-grandparents*—thought of saying. And discarded.

Aren't you now, haven't you had feelings in yourself so strong they had to come out some way? ("what howls restrained by decorum")—thought of say-ing. And discarded.

Repeat Alva: *hope ... every word out of their own life. A place to let go. And church is home.* And discarded.

The special history of the Negro people—*history?*—*just you try living what must be lived every day*—thought of saying. And discarded.

And said nothing.

And said nothing.

And soothed and held.

"Mother, a lot of the teachers and kids don't like Parry when they don't even know what she's like. Just because ..." Rocking again, convulsive and shamed. "And I'm not really her friend any more."

No news. Betrayal and shame. Who betrayed? Whose shame? Brought herself to say aloud: "But may be friends again. As Alva and I are."

The sobbing a whisper. "That girl Vicky who got that way when I fainted, she's in school. She's the one keeps wearing the lipstick and they wipe it off and she's always in trouble and now maybe she's expelled. Mother."

"Yes, lambie."

"She acts so awful outside but I remember how she was in church and whenever I see her now I have to wonder. And hear…like I'm her, Mother, like I'm her. Clinging and trembling. "Oh why do I have to feel it happens to me too?

"Mother, I want to forget about it all, and not care,—like Melanie. Why can't I forget? Oh why is it like it is and why do I have to care?"

Caressing, quieting.

Thinking: *caring asks doing. It is a long baptism into the seas of humankind, my daughter. Better immersion than to live untouched.… Yet how will you sustain?*

Why is it like it is?

Sheltering her daughter close, mourning the illusion of the embrace.

And why do I have to care?

While in her, her own need leapt and plunged for the place of strength that was not—where one could scream or sorrow while all knew and accepted, and gloved and loving hands waited to support and understand.

For Margaret Heaton, who always taught
1956

Guides to Reflection

1. Olsen includes significant portions of the minister's sermon in "O Yes." She notes that Carol, thinking of happy days in the past with Parry, does not listen much, but the readers hear the minister's vision of the "Nature of God" *(Reader, 144)*. Consider how the minister describes God and what this vision of God might mean to the parishioners.

2. When Parry's mother, Alva, speaks to Carol after she faints, she attempts to explain to Carol why her fellow parishioners worship as they do: "Not everybody feels religion the same way. Some it's in their mouth, but some it's like a hope in their blood, their bones" *(Reader, 148)*. Respond to this statement. Olsen then includes an account of a religious vision Alva had as a teenager. What purpose did the vision serve in Alva's life? Review Alva's vision at the end of part 1 *(Reader, 149)*. Note Alva's description of herself as "sin-sick" and still somewhat skeptical. How do biblical and contemporary images intermingle in the vision?

3. At several points in the story, Carol sees, thinks, or talks about Vicky, a black student at her school. At the end of the story, Carol is particularly disturbed by her memory of Vicky at Parry's church and by the fact that Vicky will most likely be expelled from school. Why do you think Olsen includes Vicky in the story? How does Vicky's experience both mirror and differ from Parry's experience?

4. "O Yes" was first published in 1957, but Olsen has claimed that the issues it raises remain relevant even after the significant changes the Civil Rights movement brought to the United States in the 1960s.[1] Do you see the problems of racial and class "sorting" that Olsen depicts in "O Yes" as characteristic of contemporary American society? If so, how?

Notes

1. Mickey Pearlman and Abby H. P. Werlock, *Tillie Olsen* (Boston: Twayne, 1991), 77.

Discover God's Presence
in Contemporary Literature

Never before has a resource touched upon the issues of life and faith in such a personal way. Excellent contemporary literature helps one realize the presence of God in many places and relationships. Each volume of *Listening for God* includes excerpts from the works of eight contemporary authors, supplemented by author profiles and reflection questions. Volumes 1 and 2 each have a companion video with interviews introducing the authors featured in the Reader. A Leader Guide, offering suggestions for organizing class time and responding to reflection questions, is packaged with each video and is also available separately. *Contributing editors: Paula J. Carlson and Peter S. Hawkins.*

Listening for God, Volume 1
Reader, Volume 1: • 0-8066-2715-8
Wonderful selections from Flannery O'Connor, Frederick Buechner, Patricia Hampl, Raymond Carver, Annie Dillard, Alice Walker, Garrison Keillor, and Richard Rodriguez.
Leader Guide, Volume 1 • 0-8066-2716-6
Videocassette, Volume 1 • 0-8066-2717-4

Listening for God, Volume 2
Reader, Volume 2: • 0-8066-2844-8
Discover new ideas and insights in selections from John Updike, Anne Tyler, Henry Louis Gates, Jr., Tobias Wolff, Carol Bly, Gail Godwin, Kathleen Norris, and Andre Dubois.
Leader Guide, Volume 2 • 0-8066-2845-6
Videocassette, Volume 2 • 0-8066-2846-4

Listening for God, Volume 3
Reader, Volume 3: • 0-8066-3962-8
This newest volume includes selections from John Cheever, Mary Gordon, Wendell Berry, Oscar Hijuelos, Reynolds Price, Louise Erdrich, Tess Gallagher, and Tillie Olsen.
Leader Guide, Volume 3 • 0-8066-3963-6